DESIGN

# 1957
# —1988

*'Courier' electric shaver*, 1963
Kenneth Grange [p.53] →

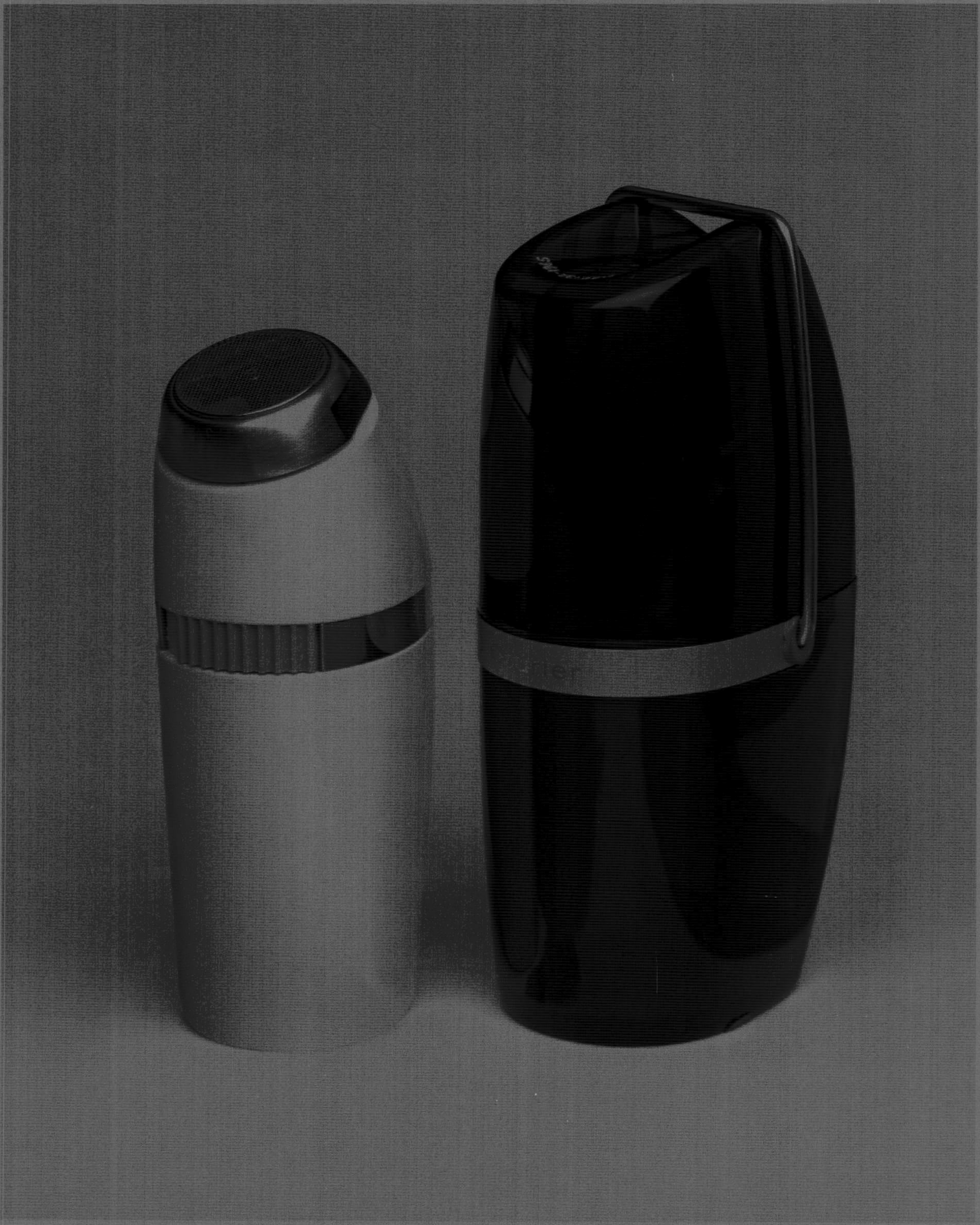

# AWARD WINNING BRITISH DESIGN

*Lily Crowther*

# 1957 —1988

V&A Publishing

First published by V&A Publishing, 2012
Victoria and Albert Museum
South Kensington
London SW7 2RL
www.vandabooks.com

Distributed in North America by Harry N. Abrams Inc., New York
© The Board of Trustees of the Victoria and Albert Museum, 2012

Hardback edition
ISBN 978 1 85177 673 3

Library of Congress Control Number 2011935130

10 9 8 7 6 5 4 3 2 1
2015 2014 2013 2012

Design: Peter & Paul

Front cover illustration: 'Bird' bath toy, from a range of toys designed
by Patrick Rylands for Trendon Ltd, 1969.

Front cover logo, pp.1 and 3: Graphic designer Hans Schleger designed this
arrow and eye symbol for the Design Centre in 1955. Reproduced courtesy
of the Estate of Hans Schleger and the Design Council.

Design Council Slide Collection at Manchester Metropolitan University/
© Design Council: pp.6–9, 10 (top), 13, 15 (centre), 17 (right), 18 (right), 19 (left),
20, 21 (left and bottom), 28, 29, 31, 35 (right), 36, 37, 43, 44, 48, 62 (top), 64,
65, 67, 75, 78–80, 81 (top), 82, 83, 85–87, 88 (bottom), 89, 93, 94 (top),
97–99, 100 (top), 101, 102, 103 (bottom), 104, 105 (right), 106 (left) and 107.

The Royal Collection © 2012 Her Majesty Elizabeth II: p.61.

V&A Photography by the V&A Photographic Studio

Printed in China

**V&A Publishing**

Supporting the world's leading
museum of art and design,
the Victoria and Albert
Museum, London

## Contents

6      The Awards: An Introduction

14     The Winning Designs: Year by Year

22 – 107    The Winning Designs: Highlights

33     Furniture/Textiles/Wallpapers and Tiles/Lighting

69     Tableware/Product Design/Toys/Jewellery

105    Audiovisual and Electronic Equipment/ Transport/Public Spaces

108    Further Reading & Acknowledgements

# The Awards:
## An Introduction

From 1957 to 1988, the UK's Council of Industrial Design (later the Design Council) conferred annual awards on British manufacturers in recognition of each year's best examples of design products, from cutlery and cameras to fitted kitchens and street lights. Despite changing names four times over the course of its existence — beginning life as the Designs of the Year, followed by the Design Centre Awards, the Council of Industrial Design Awards and finally the Design Council Awards — the scheme remained committed to two main goals: to encourage industry to recognize the commercial potential of good design, and to educate the consumer by identifying examples of well-designed products.

Some of the winning objects have become familiar players in canonical histories of modern design — Robin Day's stacking polypropylene chairs and Jock Kinneir and Margaret Calvert's road signs, for example — while others, such as artificial ski slopes or miniature televisions, are more surprising. In the early years the awards focused on identifying and recognizing designs found primarily within domestic interiors, but products made for gardens, offices and public spaces were soon among the winners. The scope of the awards broadened further in the 1960s and '70s to include more industrial products, such as vehicles and engineering equipment, yet the objective remained the same: to identify and reward design of enduring quality.

Exterior view of the Design Centre with its glass and steel façade designed by Neville Ward, Haymarket, London, 1964

The Victoria and Albert Museum, London, collected the majority of the winning products. In line with the museum's collecting interests, contemporary curators chose not to acquire some of the larger and more engineering-based winners, but the collection nonetheless includes many of the most important names in British industry, from Wedgwood to ICI. Other regular winners were design-oriented companies such as Race Furniture, Hille, Heal's and Edinburgh Weavers. Examining this varied collection offers insight into the visual and material cultures of the mid- to late twentieth century as they evolved, and shows what successive generations of tastemakers felt to be the best of their contemporaries' work. In 1966 Paul Reilly, then Director of the Design Council, suggested that 'Posterity will be able to judge the collection more dispassionately when some future director of the Victoria and Albert Museum unveils it again 50 or 100 years hence.'[1] This publication sets out to do just this; to bring to light a collection and awards scheme that gives a remarkably broad picture of over 30 years of British design.

Interior view of the Design
Centre with fittings designed
by Robert and Roger
Nicolson, 1960

Window display of products
sold with Design Centre
labels, 1959

## The Awards

The Council of Industrial Design (CoID) was established in 1944 as part of the British government's drive towards post-war economic recovery. As a design promotion body under the Board of Trade, the CoID had three key aims: to improve the design standards of British products; to promote the best British designs to consumers at home and abroad; and to encourage retailers to stock well-designed British goods, thereby helping British companies compete with their American and European rivals. Gordon Russell, a leading furniture designer and manufacturer, became Director of the CoID in 1947 and was a major influence in identifying and establishing these priorities. In 1957 he would establish the CoID's annual awards, then simply called the Designs of the Year.

Paul Reilly took over from Russell as Director of the CoID in 1959. In the years that followed the scope of the awards gradually widened to take in objects that were not directly available in the home retail market but which were regularly encountered by the public, for example street furniture, auditorium seating and road signs. Under Reilly's leadership the Council sought to influence design beyond the domestic environment, and became more involved in advising companies on engineering matters, such as the design of industrial equipment and transport. In 1967 the awards' remit expanded to include a new category for engineering and capital goods, encompassing such objects as scientific instruments and industrial machinery. The pre-existing areas covered by the awards were grouped into a new consumer and contract goods category. The awards became the Council of Industrial Design Awards that same year, only to be renamed once again in 1972 when the CoID became the Design

Council in a formal nod to its broadening remit; the awards duly became the Design Council Awards. During the 1970s and '80s, the capital goods category was subdivided into separate categories for engineering products and components, medical equipment and the motor industry. The awards continued to be given annually until 1988, when the new Director, Ivor Owen, switched from public campaigning to focus on business and education, and the Design Council's retailing and product endorsement services were closed.

Exhibition of award-winning products at the Design Centre, including 'Pannus' wallpaper, designed by Humphrey Spender (left), 1960

The Designs of the Year had its origins in the 1951 Festival of Britain, a series of exhibitions and events across the UK celebrating British achievements past and present. The Festival's core programming centred on the Southbank, an area of central London just south of the river Thames. Here the nation's best architects and designers built pavilions to reflect patriotic themes, with such titles as 'The Land of Britain', 'The Sea and Ships' and 'Homes and Gardens'. In the lead-up to the Festival, the Industrial Division of the CoID selected and assembled objects to illustrate each pavilion's respective theme, as well as for the Festival's regional and travelling exhibitions. Led by architect Mark Hartland Thomas, a team of specialist industrial liaison and development officers travelled the country between 1947 and 1951, identifying well-designed products and encouraging the development of new designs. The results of their survey were recorded in a card index of over 20,000 exhibition-worthy products, half of which were actually shown at the Festival. The index, known as the *Design Review*, was illustrated with photographs of products and was available for consultation by visitors to the Southbank.[2]

The Festival generated widespread public interest in design, which the CoID capitalized on to raise its profile in the years that followed. On 26 April 1956, Prince Philip, Duke of Edinburgh, opened the Design Centre on London's Haymarket as the organization's new headquarters. Architect Neville Ward had designed the building's decorative façade, while Robert and Roger Nicolson had designed the interiors. As well as offices, the building provided space for the permanent display of contemporary British goods and exhibitions on particular themes or manufacturers. After 1951 the *Design Review* had become a permanent part of the CoID's work, with approved products continuously being added to the index by industrial officers. It was soon renamed the *Design Index* and it included samples of two-dimensional products, such as textiles, wallpapers and tiles, photographs of other types of products, and information related to their design, availability and prices. The public and trade buyers were encouraged to consult its contents at the Design Centre, and several new regional centres: the Scottish Design Centre in Glasgow opened in 1957, followed by the Bristol Building and Design Centre, the Manchester Design Centre and the Midland Design and Building Centre in Nottingham.

The inaugural Designs of the Year were selected from the *Design Index* by a panel of assessors drawn from the Faculty of Royal Designers for Industry. Twelve manufacturers each received an award for their respective products, which were chosen as excellent examples of design. After 1957 the adjudication process became more closely tied to the selection process for the *Design Index*. The CoID's industrial officers encouraged manufacturers to submit their designs for inclusion in the index, which automatically made them eligible to be considered for an award. Specialist committees, including both practising designers and CoID staff, met regularly to assess the entries from each industry. The committees covered traditional fields of design, such as furniture, textiles and ceramics, as well as more modern industries, such as plastics. Industrial officers could also nominate one-off handmade objects, such as pieces of fine jewellery, for consideration. When a committee came across a particularly good design, then in addition to recommending it for the index, they would add it to the longlist for the awards. A judging panel assembled from members of the committees, generally comprising about five individuals from a range of backgrounds, chose the year's award winners from this list.

Exhibition of award-winning products at the Design Centre, including a range of toys designed by Patrick Rylands for Trendon (centre), and the 'Kensington' range of Brussels carpets designed by David Hicks (right), 1970

Over the decades the awards' judging panels included distinguished designers, often award winners themselves, and such leading design consultants as Milner Gray and Misha Black of the Design Research Unit, and Jane Priestman, then the design manager for the British Airports Authority. There was also a consistently strong representation of several other professions on the panel: architects included Basil Spence, Jane Drew and Inette Austin-Smith; critics ranged from establishment architectural historians, such as John Summerson and J.M. Richards, to young journalists and design writers, for example Shirley Conran and Fiona MacCarthy; retailers included Geoffrey Dunn of the progressive department store Dunn's of Bromley, Michael Moss of Woollands, and Anthony Heal of Heal's. Academics, such as Robin Darwin, Rector of the Royal College of Art, also found places on the judging panels. While attempting to select winners from the widest possible range of industries, the judges also tried to maintain a consistently high standard, so if a particular industry produced no good designs in a given year then it would receive no awards. For example, in 1961 no textiles, carpets or wallpapers were chosen, although the following year these patterned products dominated.

A perennial difficulty in selecting award winners was the CoID's ambition to identify and reward good design objectively, rather than follow the latest trends. As early as 1958, an article in *Design*, the CoID journal, noted that 'it is desirable to distinguish the worthwhile contribution from the merely fashionable, without undervaluing the role that fashion must always play in the more decorative products.'[3] The judges of the 1964 awards noted that their chosen winners were 'conspicuously free from extraneous, ephemeral features that are sometimes introduced into products solely for their initial effect', continuing to point out that 'the real hazard now appears to be an acceptance of design standards which are ephemeral and fashionable rather than permanent and durable'.[4] This criticism alludes to the growing influence and availability of playful, disposable 'Pop' design in the early 1960s, which, with its strong appeal to younger consumers, would eventually became impossible for

Display at the Design Centre of the award-winning 'Input' range of plastic containers, designed by Conran Associates for Crayonne Ltd, 1974

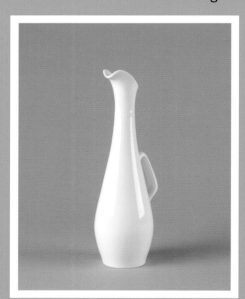

Jug from the Duke of Edinburgh prize-winning 'Apollo' range of tableware, designed by Neal French and David White for W.T. Copeland & Sons Ltd, 1960

the CoID to ignore. Paul Reilly acknowledged this fact in his 1967 article 'The Challenge of Pop', in which he suggested that 'a design may be valid at a given time for a given purpose to a given group of people in a given set of circumstances, but that outside those limits it may not be valid at all'.[5] Awards were eventually given to several 'Pop' designs, including Peter Murdoch's 'Those Things' cardboard furniture, and textiles by Barbara Brown and Shirley Craven.

A new prize was introduced in 1959: the Duke of Edinburgh's Prize for Elegant Design. Prince Philip, Duke of Edinburgh, had a long-standing interest in the CoID and had presented certificates to the award winners since the inception of the scheme in 1957. His new prize was distinguished by being awarded to a designer rather than a manufacturer. An independent panel, nominated and chaired by the Duke, normally selected just one winner each year, although occasionally two designers shared the prize. The criterion of elegance was chosen 'to encourage a positive attitude towards design as a whole',[6] and could be interpreted in an aesthetic sense as 'refinement of taste', as well as in the more technical sense of an elegant solution to a problem.[7] This flexibility in definition led to a great diversity of winners, from silk furnishing fabrics to helicopters (see The Winning Designs: Year by Year — recipients of the Duke of Edinburgh's Prize for Elegant Design are given directly after each annual subheading). Now renamed the Prince Philip Designer's Prize, it is the only surviving element of the scheme. It continues to be awarded annually, though the focus has shifted over time towards recognition of a designer's whole career and contribution to the design profession, rather than of a specific product. Recent winners include James Dyson, Terence Conran and Norman Foster.

Winning an award from the CoID could have a positive effect on sales. In 1965, 107 of the 132 award winners to date were still in production, including trend-led products, such as textiles, which might have been expected to have a shorter shelf life. Sales were particularly boosted for contract products because architects were especially aware of the awards and would specify the use of winning designs such as carpeting, door furniture and light fittings in their buildings. The committees responsible for approving architects' specifications tended to be reassured by the use of products with the official approval of the CoID.[8] Retail sales were helped by the special labels that manufacturers were entitled to use on point-of-sale displays and packaging for products included in the *Design Index*. Award-winning products sold better than comparable products in their range, which manufacturers attributed to the extra publicity provided by the press coverage of the awards.[9] The CoID sought to raise the scheme's profile by holding the annual awards ceremony in important new buildings around the country. In 1969 it took place on board the *Queen Elizabeth II*, or *QE2*, a flagship ocean liner launched by Cunard that year. Each year an annual exhibition of the winners opened at the Design Centre, and satellite displays toured the country. These touring shows ranged from major exhibitions at such venues as the Scottish Design Centre to small displays of winning objects in shops. Mounted sets of photographs of the winners were circulated to libraries and art colleges.

A central ambition since the scheme's inception had been to improve the reputation of British design and designers in overseas markets. In 1957 Walter Worboys, Chairman of the CoID, argued: 'To have a reputation for producing well-made and well-designed goods is a valuable commercial asset, and one which will be particularly important when the opening of the European Free Trade Area [in 1960] will offer us a large and sophisticated market for exploitation.'[10] His assessment proved apt: from the huge multinational Kodak to small mathematical-instruments specialist Thornton, companies found that winning an award encouraged European consumers and competitors to take their British-designed products more seriously. In 1977 almost three-quarters of the winning companies reported that the award had helped them to increase sales abroad.[11] James Pilditch, chairman of the consultancy Allied Industrial Designers, noted that same year that 'the correlation between good design … and exports is profoundly important: a self-sufficient justification, if one was needed, of the Design Council and the Government funds that support it.'[12] His endorsement of the Design Council's value responded to the difficult economic situation of the late 1970s, a period of prolonged recession when manufacturing in Britain declined substantially.

### The V&A: Collecting Award-Winning Design

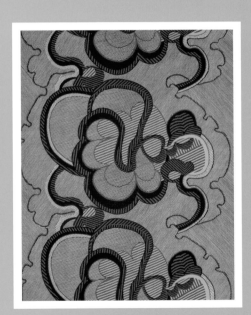

Award-winning 'Simple Solar' furnishing fabric, designed by Shirley Craven for Hull Traders Ltd, 1966

The Council of Industrial Design and the Victoria and Albert Museum shared a common interest in informing and inspiring design practitioners and in educating the wider public on design. There was a particular affinity between the CoID and the V&A's Circulation Department, as the latter had been established in order to generate touring exhibitions with an emphasis on recent and contemporary work from established designers, leading colleges and progressive companies. Unlike other curatorial departments, Circulation was therefore very active in contemporary collecting and its shows toured to regional museums, art colleges and other educational institutions around Britain. In the late 1940s, Gordon Russell held extended discussions with Leigh Ashton, then Director of the V&A, and a non-voting member of the CoID since 1945, and Peter Floud, then Keeper of the Circulation Department, about the possibility of establishing a permanent gallery of contemporary industrial design at the museum, in time for the Festival of Britain. The gallery was to be housed on a purpose-built mezzanine level above the museum's North Court galleries, and its displays would be selected and regularly refreshed by the CoID. This ambitious plan was not realized at the time, but in 1953 Ashton was still hoping to update the V&A's galleries of British design with 'a room of modern exhibits which could suitably act as a shop window for our Department of Circulation'.[13]

When the CoID's awards scheme was established in 1957, Russell hoped to display the winners at the V&A, and anticipated that the museum might acquire them for its permanent collection. He suggested this idea to Trenchard Cox, who had succeeded Ashton as Director of the V&A in 1955, and who Russell afterwards said was 'obviously very interested ... although he personally did not like some of them'.[14] Cox discussed the idea with Floud, and they agreed that it would only be worthwhile if the museum committed itself to acquiring all of the winners each year in order to build up a representative collection; however, they were cautious about imposing this potentially onerous and unpredictable commitment on their successors.

Floud suggested to Russell that he would be prepared to acquire each year's winners as long as the V&A could 'limit our acceptance to objects which could be regarded as forming part of the normal equipment of a living room', meaning that they would 'decline items such as vehicles, refrigerators, washing-machines, boilers, office equipment etc, should they be selected'.[15] He explained that 'although it might appear logical to the theorist, the average person would not expect to find washing machines in the same building as, for example, Renaissance sculpture'.[16] Russell agreed to this policy in principle, and was prepared to allow the museum to choose those objects most relevant to its purposes; however, Cox and his staff continued to feel that someone should be collecting all of the objects in a systematic way, instead of picking and choosing, and concluded that the V&A was not in a position to do this. Thus nothing came of this initial attempt to establish a collection.

The discussion was revived in 1960 by Paul Reilly, the new CoID Director, James Noel White, his deputy, and Hugh Wakefield, the new Keeper of the Circulation Department, who were conscious that as the years passed it would become increasingly difficult to gather up a complete collection of previous winners. Though Cox remained concerned that some of the objects were unsuitable for the V&A — and tried unsuccessfully to persuade the Science Museum to share responsibility for the collection[17] — Wakefield pressed ahead securing storage space and making other practical arrangements. Collecting officially began in 1962, apparently thanks largely to Wakefield's determination. By the end of 1963, the museum had succeeded in gathering together almost all of the winners from the first seven years of the awards scheme.

Despite Wakefield's reassurance to Cox that he 'would leave it open to us to avoid any quite exceptionally unsuitable objects', his collecting strategy was in fact remarkably catholic.[18] Over the next 15 years, the V&A acquired the great majority of winning products, including some which fell well outside Floud's original restrictions. When the capital goods category was introduced in 1967, the museum decided not to collect these objects, and reserved the right to exclude some especially large consumer award winners, such as boats; nonetheless, the collection does feature objects not traditionally associated with museums of art and design, including a dishwasher, a post franking machine, a chemical toilet and a bicycle. The determined and systematic collecting activity of the Circulation Department was supported by staff at the CoID, who took responsibility for encouraging each winning manufacturer or designer to send examples of their products to the museum. Often the museum acquired a small number of objects to represent larger award-winning groups; for example, a tea service may be represented in the collection by just the teapot and milk jug. Sometimes several objects were collected to represent a single winning design; these may include variant colours, cutaway models or design drawings.

Exhibition of award-winning products at the Design Centre, including 'Chinese Ivory' cutlery designed by David Mellor (left), and the 'Topper' sailing dinghy designed by Ian Proctor (right), 1977

The collection in itself became an incentive for designers to enter their products for an award. As Noel Jordan of Race Furniture reflected: 'The fact that all Design Centre Awards are kept by the Victoria & Albert Museum means that in 100 years' time, the products you thought about and worked on will still exist and this, I think, is a tremendous thrill.'[19] The crucial importance of Circulation to this collecting programme is demonstrated by what happened when the department closed in 1977: only 5% of the winners were acquired in the following decade.[20] Despite this drop-off in collecting, nearly two-thirds of all the winning designs are represented in the V&A's permanent collections, almost all of them collected by the Circulation Department.

## Notes

1. Paul Reilly, 'Ten Years of Design Centre Awards', *Design*, May 1966, p.59

2. For an extended discussion of the CoID's role in the Festival of Britain, see Paul Reilly's 'The Role of the Design Council Before, During and After the Festival of Britain', Mary Banham and Bevis Hillier (eds.), *A Tonic to the Nation: the Festival of Britain 1951* (London, 1976), pp.58-61

3. 'The Judges' Report', *Design*, June 1958, p.23

4. 'Design Centre Awards 1964', *Design*, June 1964, p.38

5. Paul Reilly, 'The Challenge of Pop', *Architectural Review*, vol. 142, no. 848, 1967, pp.255—7

6. Prince Philip, Duke of Edinburgh, quoted in 'Prince Philip at the Design Centre: the Elegance Prize and Designs of the Year, 1959'. University of Brighton Design Archives: Design Council Archive, Council of Industrial Design Press Release IDG 569:15.5.59, 15 May 1959

7. 'Designs of the Year 1959', *Design*, June 1959, p.32

8. Richard Carr, 'The Award Winners Speak Out', *Design*, May 1966, p.72. See also Paul Reilly, 'Conscience of Industry', *The Ambassador*, October 1965, pp.99—102

9. 'The Rewards of Awards', *Design*, June 1965, p.29

10. Quoted in 'Designs of the Year: Prince Philip at the Design Centre'. University of Brighton Design Archives: Design Council Archive, Council of Industrial Design Press Release IDG 44975501, 10 May 1957, p.2

11. Richard Carr, 'The Award Winners Speak Out', *Design*, May 1966, p.73, and James Pilditch, 'The Story So Far', *Design*, April 1977, p.28

12. James Pilditch, 'The Story So Far', *Design*, April 1977, pp.28—31

13. Letter from Leigh Ashton to Gordon Russell, 14 January 1953. University of Brighton Design Archives: Design Council Archive, file DCA/118. The proposed mezzanine was eventually built in 1957 to serve as a paintings gallery; it later became the twentieth-century furniture study gallery, and now houses the theatre and performance collections. See John Physick, *The Victoria and Albert Museum: The History of its Building* (London, 1982), pp.271—2

14. Letter from Gordon Russell to J. Noel White, 16 April 1957. University of Brighton Design Archives: Design Council Archive, file DCA/118

15. Letter from Peter Floud to Gordon Russell, 31 May 1957. V&A Archive, file MA/1/D981/2. (Duplicated in University of Brighton Design Archives: Design Council Archive, file DCA/118.)

16. Letter from Peter Floud to Gordon Russell, 15 August 1957. V&A Archive, file MA/1/D981/2. (Duplicated in University of Brighton Design Archives: Design Council Archive, file DCA/118.)

17. Letter from David Follett, Director of the Science Museum, to Trenchard Cox, 24 February 1961. V&A Archive, file MA/1/D981/2

18. Note from Hugh Wakefield to Trenchard Cox, 12 June 1961. V&A Archive, file MA/1/D981/2

19. Quoted in Richard Carr, 'The Award Winners Speak Out', *Design*, May 1966, p.73

20. The Circulation Department, briefly renamed Regional Services, was closed due to government funding cuts. Its objects were dispersed amongst the museum's materials-based collections departments.

# The Winning Designs: Year by Year

These designs were recognized with a Designs of the Year award (1957–9), a Design Centre Award (1960–66), a Council of Industrial Design Award (1967–71), or a Design Council Award (1972–88). The list is chronological by year and includes the designer and manufacturing information where known. Where appropriate the entry gives the relevant V&A object number(s).

From 1957 to 1967, the list includes all the award-winning products in all categories; after 1967, it includes only products within the consumer and contract goods categories. Beginning in 1959, one object was recognized each year with the Duke of Edinburgh's Prize for Elegant Design: all these objects, even if they fall outside the consumer and contract goods categories, are listed below.

### 1957

'Convertible' sofa bed, upholstered mattress on a metal frame, designed by Robin Day for S. Hille & Co.
V&A: Circ.508–1968

'CS17' 17-inch television and stand, wooden cabinet on steel stand, designed by Robin Day (cabinet) and J.E. Cope (circuit) for Pye Ltd
V&A: Circ.231&A–1963

'Imperial' Axminster broadloom carpet, wool, designed by Lucienne Day for Tomkinsons Ltd
V&A: Circ.472–1963

'Pride' cutlery, electro-plated nickel silver; the knives have stainless steel blades and white composition handles; designed by David Mellor for Walker & Hall Ltd
V&A: Circ.292-J–1959

'PO200' pendant lampshade, cellulose acetate, designed by John and Sylvia Reid for Rotaflex Ltd
V&A: Circ.387–1963

**'Melmex' tableware, melamine, designed by A.H. Woodfull and John D. Vale of the Product Design Service, British Industrial Plastics Ltd, manufactured by Streetly Manufacturing Co. for W.R. Midwinter Ltd**
**V&A: Circ.450 to 453–1963**

'Rayburn' convector heater, designed by David Ogle for Allied Iron Founders Ltd
V&A: Circ.217–1963

'Connoisseur' wine glasses, glass, designed by Sven Fogelberg for Thomas Webb & Sons
V&A: Circ.430-C–1963

'Strawberry Hill' dinner and tea ware, bone china with printed and gilded decoration, designed by Victor Skellern and Millicent Taplin for Josiah Wedgwood & Sons Ltd
V&A: Circ.435 to 437–1963

'Flamingo' furnishing fabric, printed cotton, designed by Tibor Reich for Tibor Ltd
V&A: Circ.463&A–1963

'Impasto' wallpaper, printed paper. From the 'Palladio' range, designed by Audrey Levy for The Wall Paper Manufacturers Ltd
V&A: Circ.295–1963, E.445:8-9–1988

'Pyrex' ovenware, heat-resistant glass, designed by John D. Cochrane with Milner Gray and Kenneth Lamble of the Design Research Unit, for James A. Jobling & Co.

### 1958

'Phantom Rose' wallpaper, screen-printed paper. From the 'Palladio 2' range, designed by Audrey Levy for The Wall Paper Manufacturers Ltd
V&A: Circ.296–1963

'Conference' tableware, earthenware with printed decoration. Pattern designed by Pat Albeck, 'Metro' shape designed by Tom Arnold, for Ridgway Potteries Ltd
V&A: Circ.438 to 441–1963

'Old Hall' toast rack, stainless steel, designed by Robert Welch for J. & J. Wiggin Ltd
V&A: Circ.419–1963

'Adam' furnishing fabric, jacquard-woven cotton and rayon, designed by Keith Vaughan for Edinburgh Weavers
V&A: Circ.466–1963

'Minster' furnishing fabric, printed cotton satin, designed by Humphrey Spender for Edinburgh Weavers
V&A: Circ.467&A–1963

'Queensberry' ovenware, enamelled cast iron, designed by David Queensberry for Enamelled Iron & Steel Products Co.

'Vistavu' slide viewer, designed by Harold R. Stapleton, assisted by Howard Upjohn, for Rank Precision Industries Ltd

'Hiflo' bibcock tap, brass, designed by company design staff under W. Petzall at Barking Brassware Co. Ltd
V&A: Circ.415–1963

'Prestwick' suitcases and overnight cases, leather, designed by Kenneth H. Paterson for S.E. Norris & Co. Ltd
V&A: Circ.222–1963

**'Gold Seal Superbath' baby bath, polythene with wooden stand, designed by Martyn Rowlands for Ekco Plastics Ltd**
**V&A: Circ.230:1&2–1963**

'Artkurl' Wilton curled-pile broadloom carpet, wool, designed by company design staff under James Galloway at William C. Gray & Sons Ltd
V&A: Circ.469-D–1963

'Taperback' occasional chair, welded steel frame and upholstered seat, designed by John Neville Stafford for Stafford Furniture Ltd
V&A: Circ.228–1963

'Knifecut' pruner, designed by Hulme Chadwick with company design staff at Wilkinson Sword Ltd
V&A: Circ.413–1963

'Satina' pendant light fitting, metal rods with brass connectors and opal glass shades, designed by Nigel Chapman, manufactured by Hailwood & Ackroyd Ltd for AEI Lamp & Lighting Co. Ltd
V&A: Circ.389-C–1963

'Hamilton' sideboard, rosewood and cherry wood, designed by Robert Heritage for Archie Shine Ltd
V&A: Circ.227–1963

'Royal Gobelin' Axminster body carpet, wool, designed by Neville and Mary Ward of Ward & Austin for Tomkinsons Ltd

'Riviera' tablecloths and napkins, woven cotton, designed by Arthur Ingham for John Shields & Co. (Perth) Ltd
V&A: Circ.464-F–1963

'Carlton' wash basin, ceramic, designed by company design staff under James E. Gray at Shanks & Co. Ltd
V&A: Circ.226–1963

'Vision Net' curtaining, cotton machine lace reinforced with Terylene, designed by F.G. Hobden with company design staff at Clyde Manufacturing Co.

'Tallent' paraffin oil convector heater, designed by company design staff under Cecil T. Howard at Tallent (Aycliffe) Ltd
V&A: Circ.229–1963

### 1959

Duke of Edinburgh's Prize for Elegant Design: 'Packaway' refrigerator, steel with anodized aluminium cover strip and chromium finished handle, designed by C.W.F. Longman with Edward Wilkes for Pressed Steel Company Ltd (Prestcold Division)

'Mandala' Wilton carpet, wool, designed by Audrey Tanner for Carpet Manufacturing Co. Ltd
V&A: Circ.470&A–1963

'Pride' tea service, electro-plated nickel silver with nylon handles, designed by David Mellor for Walker & Hall Ltd
V&A: Circ.293&A–1959

'Flamingo' easy chair, foam rubber padding and wool upholstery over steel frame with wooden legs and plastic feet, designed by Ernest Race for Race Furniture Ltd
V&A: Circ.223–1963

'Malindi' furnishing fabric, printed cotton satin, designed by Gwenfred Jarvis for Liberty & Co.
V&A: Circ.462-B—1963

Fluorescent kitchen light, designed by John and Sylvia Reid for Atlas Lighting Ltd
V&A: Circ.380—1963

'Planit' wall tiles, silk-screened ceramic, designed by Derek Hodgkinson for H. & R. Johnson Ltd
V&A: Circ.390:1-60—1963

'DG1' circular dining table, laminated wood, designed by Hassan El-Hayani, manufactured by Design Furniture Ltd for New Furniture Design Group

'Piazza', plastic-coated textile, designed by Edward Pond for Bernard Wardle (Everflex) Ltd
V&A: Circ.461&A—1963

'Queen-heater' solid fuel room heater, designed by David Mellor for Grahamston Iron Co. Ltd
V&A: Circ.218—1963

'Swoe' garden tool, metal blade with rubber handle, designed by Hulme Chadwick with company design staff at Wilkinson Sword Ltd
V&A: Circ.454—1963

'K.42.R' lever door handle, aluminium, designed by Roger Peach for Dryad Metal Works Ltd
V&A: Circ.411—1963

'KI' professional tripod, designed by Walter Kennedy for Kennedy Instruments Ltd
V&A: Circ.220—1963

'Ellipse' series light fitting, aluminium rod and reflector, and opal glass shade, designed by Paul Boissevain for Merchant Adventurers Ltd
V&A: Circ.388—1963

'Aristocrat' socket chisels, steel shaft with plastic or beech handle, designed by company engineering staff under John A. Hattersley at Ward & Payne Ltd
V&A: Circ.297-G—1963

'Inglewood' furnishing fabric, jacquard-woven cotton and rayon, designed by Humphrey Spender for Edinburgh Weavers
V&A: Circ.357-B—1958, Circ.465—1963, T.369—2009

## 1960

Duke of Edinburgh's Prize for Elegant Design: 'Apollo' dinner, tea and coffee ware, initially known as 'Royal College Shape', bone china, designed by Neal French and David White for W.T. Copeland & Sons Ltd
V&A: Circ.391 to 410—1963

Street lighting columns and lanterns, designed by Richard Stevens and manufactured by Abacus Engineering Ltd for Atlas Lighting Ltd
V&A: Circ.376 to 379—1963, TN.289—2011

**'Queensberry Ware' nursery tableware, bone china with printed decoration. Shape designed by David Queensberry; pattern designed by Bernard Blatch for Crown Staffordshire China Co. Ltd**
**V&A: Circ.416 to 418—1963**

'Orlando' furnishing fabric, woven stripe linen and cotton, designed by company design staff under Peter Simpson at Donald Brothers Ltd
V&A: Circ.473 & 474—1963

**'Chelsea' light fittings, metal and hand-blown coloured glass, designed by Richard Stevens and Peter Rodd for Atlas Lighting Ltd, with shades made by James Powell & Sons (Whitefriars Glassworks) Ltd**
**V&A: Circ.382-F—1963, Circ.383-B—1963**

'Brownie 44a' camera, metal casing with leather-covered plastic side panels, designed by Kenneth Grange with company staff under F.H.G. Pitt at Kodak Ltd
V&A: Circ.414—1963

'Fiesta' plates, melamine, designed by Ronald E. Brookes for Brookes & Adams Ltd
V&A: Circ.421 to 429—1963

'Royal Gobelin' Axminster carpet, wool, designed by Graham Tutton for Tomkinsons Ltd
V&A: Circ.471—1963

'Formation Furniture' office desk units, abura with black linoleum tops and white PVC apron panels, designed by Brian Henderson of Yorke, Rosenberg & Mardall for Bath Cabinet Makers Ltd

'Le Bosquet' furnishing fabric, printed cotton satin, designed by Shirley Craven for Hull Traders Ltd
V&A: Circ.460—1963, T.141—1989

'Anniversary Ware' casseroles, dishes and stands, vitreous enamelled cast iron, designed by John and Sylvia Reid for Izons & Co. Ltd
V&A: Circ.445 to 449—1963

'Lemington' vases, glass, designed by Ronald Stennett-Wilson for Osram Glassworks (GEC)
V&A: Circ.443 & 444—1963

'Bouquet Garni', 'Too Many Cooks' and 'Black Leaf' glass towels, printed Irish linen, designed by Lucienne Day for Thomas Somerset & Co. Ltd
V&A: Circ.455 to 457—1963

'Judge' saucepans, stainless steel, designed by Misha Black and Ronald Armstrong of the Design Research Unit for Ernest Stevens Ltd

Low-voltage display spotlight, anodized aluminium, designed by Richard Stevens for Atlas Lighting Ltd
V&A: Circ.381—1963

'Denison Vision Net' furnishing lace, cotton and Terylene, designed by F.G. Hobden for Clyde Manufacturing Co.
V&A: Circ.459—1963

'Vynide', PVC-coated textile, designed by company design staff under Frank J. Hoswell at ICI (Hyde) Ltd
V&A: Circ.468—1963

'Pannus' wallpaper, screen-printed paper. From the 'Palladio Magnus' range, designed by Humphrey Spender for The Wall Paper Manufacturers Ltd
V&A: Circ.292&A—1963, E.443—1988

## 1961

Duke of Edinburgh's Prize for Elegant Design: 'Rio TR70' transistor radio, polystyrene cabinet and aluminium grille, designed by Eric Marshall for Ultra Radio & Television Ltd
V&A: Circ.293—1963

'Monte Carlo' carving set, stainless steel and carbon steel, designed by Geoffrey Bellamy for George Wostenholm & Son Ltd
V&A: Circ.420-B—1963

'Form' unit furniture, makore with steel base frames and plastic laminate or mahogany veneer tops, designed by Robin Day for S. Hille & Co. Ltd

'Orbit' furniture castors, stove-enamelled zinc alloy and mild steel, designed by R. David Carter with company design staff at Joseph Gillott & Sons
V&A: Circ.294—1963

'Town Number One' litter bin, perforated sheet steel with a steel base, designed by Derek Goad and John Ricks of Donald Forrest for G.A. Harvey & Co. (London) Ltd
V&A: Circ.219—1963

'Kodaslide 40' slide projector, polystyrene casing, designed by Kenneth Grange with company staff at Kodak Ltd
V&A: Circ.412—1963

'PC180' table mirror, brass frame and stove-enamelled steel stand, designed by Colin Beales for Peter Cuddon
V&A: Circ.533—1963

'PC181' towel rail, porcelain with a nickel-plated steel core and aluminium frame, designed and manufactured by Peter Cuddon

**'Cormorant' folding outdoor chair, laminated mahogany seat and afromosia frame, designed by Ernest Race for Race Furniture Ltd**
**V&A: Circ.224—1963**

'Paragon' chemical toilet, polythene with nylon hinges and stainless steel handle, designed by Martyn Rowlands for Racasan Ltd
V&A: Circ.225—1963

'Redfyre Centramatic 35' oil-fired boiler, stove enamelled with anodized aluminium front panel, designed by Brian Asquith with company design staff at Newton, Chambers & Co. Ltd
V&A: Circ.221—1963

Adjustable spotlights, anodized aluminium lamp housing with vitreous enamelled base plate, designed by John and Sylvia Reid for Rotaflex (Great Britain) Ltd
V&A: Circ.384 to 386—1963

'Chef Royal' saucepans, vitreous enamelled steel with plastic handles and chromium plated rims, designed by Berkeley Associates for Edward Curran Engineering Ltd
V&A: Circ.431 to 434—1963

## 1962

Duke of Edinburgh's Prize for Elegant Design:
'Grisette', 'Tanjong', 'Ali Baba', 'Aladdin', 'Domenica',
'Charade', 'Solace', 'Rocha', 'Quip', 'Maestro' and
'Harmony' furnishing fabrics, woven silk, acetate
and rayon, designed by Nicholas Sekers for West
Cumberland Silk Mills Ltd
V&A: Circ.600-B—1963

Gramophone precision pick-up arm, chrome-plated
stainless steel with wood lining and plastic shell,
designed by A. Robertson-Aikman and
W.J. Watkinson for SME Ltd
V&A: Circ.589—1963

'Trifoliate' wallpaper, screen-printed paper. From
the 'Palladio 5' range, designed by Cliff Holden for
The Wall Paper Manufacturers Ltd
V&A: Circ.596-B—1963

'Symbol' cutlery, stainless steel, designed
by David Mellor for Walker & Hall Ltd
V&A: Circ.593-F—1963

**'Sunflower' furnishing fabric, screen-printed
crêpe-weave cotton, designed by Howard
Carter for Heal Fabrics Ltd
V&A: Circ.3—1962, Circ.598 & 599-G—1963,
T.299:1-4—1999**

Hoe and rake, stainless steel heads with aluminium
handles and melamine knobs, designed by Brian
Asquith for Spear & Jackson Ltd
V&A: Circ.594 & 595—1963

'Cawdor' furnishing fabric, linen, designed by
company design staff under Peter Simpson at
Donald Brothers Ltd
V&A: Circ.597-C—1963

Dimpled wall tiles, glazed Dimex ceramic body,
designed by Michael Caddy for Wade Architectural
Ceramics
V&A: Circ.590-W—1963

'BR' heavy-duty settee, moulded beech ply seat and
back on a steel frame, upholstered in vinyl fabric or
leather, designed by Robin Day for S. Hille & Co. Ltd

'Vacco de Luxe VLP' vacuum flask, polythene casing,
designed by L. Leslie-Smith for Vacco Ltd
V&A: Circ.591 & 592—1963

'Old Hall' dishes, stainless steel, designed by Robert
Welch for J. & J. Wiggin Ltd

## 1963

Duke of Edinburgh's Prize for Elegant Design:
'Courier' cordless electric shaver, steel cutter
screen mounted in chromium-plated brass with
melamine casing and cellulose acetate carrying
case, designed by Kenneth Grange for Henry
Milward & Sons
V&A: Circ.132—1965, Circ.833—1966

'Heritage A.K.' wall storage units, pine, designed
by Robert Heritage for Archie Shine Ltd
V&A: Circ.136:1-7—1965

'Lightweight' slide storage box, strawboard with
linen-reinforced hinges and plastic inner tray,
designed by Albert H. Cragg for Boots Pure Drug
Co. Ltd
V&A: Circ.130&A—1965

'Cruachan' furnishing fabric, hand screen-printed
cotton satin, designed by Peter McCulloch for Hull
Traders Ltd
V&A: Circ.122-B—1965, T.174—1989

'Harrington' furnishing fabric, machine-printed
cotton, designed by Humphrey Spender for Cepea
Fabrics Ltd
V&A: Circ.131&A—1965

'Sheppey' settees and chair, upholstered over stove-
enamelled steel frames with English ash end frames,
designed by Ernest Race for Race Furniture Ltd
V&A: Circ.115—1965

Trays and hors d'oeuvre dishes, acrylic polymethyl
methacrylate, designed by Noel Lefebvre for Xlon
Products
V&A: Circ.133-B—1965

Pay-on-answer coin-operated phone, stove-
enamelled pressure-cast aluminium casing with
stainless steel fittings. Case designed by Douglas
Scott; engineering designed by Associated
Automation Ltd with the General Post Office,
manufactured by Associated Automation Ltd
V&A: Circ.134—1965

Stacking chair, steamed beech frame upholstered
in PVC, designed by Clive Bacon for Design
Furnishing Contracts Ltd
V&A: Circ.135&A—1965

'Oregon' dining chair, pine frame upholstered with
'Everflex' or Tibor 'Regent' material, designed by
Robert Heritage for Archie Shine Ltd
V&A: Circ.114—1965

'Corinthian' 3 kW electric fire, anodized aluminium
reflector and cast aluminium surround and frame,
designed by David Brunton for Belling & Co. Ltd
V&A: Circ.129—1965

'Sola' wash basin, Ceramant vitreous ceramic,
designed by E. Stanley Ellis for Twyfords Ltd
V&A: Circ.113—1965

## 1964

Duke of Edinburgh's Prize for Elegant Design:
'Diadem', 'Harlequin', 'Random' and 'Mitre' ranges
of cut glassware, hand-formed and decorated lead
crystal, designed by David Queensberry for Webb
Corbett Ltd
V&A: Circ.127-D—1965, Circ.1163—1967

'Lamina' wallpaper, screen-printed paper. From
the 'Palladio' range, designed by Deryck Healey
for The Wall Paper Manufacturers Ltd
V&A: Circ.128-C—1965

Range of electric doorbells and fittings, acrylic and
polystyrene cases and phosphor bronze contacts,
designed by Norman Stevenson with company
design staff at V. & E. Friedland Ltd
V&A: Circ.120—1965

**'Moulton Stowaway' bicycle, mild steel frame and
rubber suspension, designed by Alex Moulton for
Moulton Bicycles Ltd
V&A: Circ.125—1965**

'Brompton' chair, afromosia or beech frame with
plywood back and 'Cirrus' PVC-covered fabric
upholstery, designed by Ronald Carter for Dancer
& Hearne Bros Ltd
V&A: Circ.14—1966

'Nubian' laminate, rotogravure printed plastic,
designed by Helen Dalby for Formica Ltd

'Glendale' woven fabrics, linen blended with rayon
and cotton, designed by William Robertson and
Peter Simpson for Donald Bros Ltd
V&A: Circ.116-T—1965

'Memory' master clock, steel and brass mechanism
in mahogany case with aluminium dial and bezel.
Case and dial designed by Robert Heritage;
mechanism designed by company design staff at
English Clock Systems Ltd
V&A: Circ.118—1965

**'Brownie Vecta' camera, plastic body with nickel-
plated fittings, designed by Kenneth Grange with
company design staff at Kodak Ltd
V&A: Circ.124—1965**

Insulated tumbler, styrene acrylonitrile with metallic
coating on the inner surface, designed by H.D.F.
Creighton for Insulex Ltd
V&A: Circ.123-B—1965

Garden shears, steel blades with plastic-coated
aluminium tangs and beech handles, designed by
Hulme Chadwick with company design staff at
Wilkinson Sword Ltd
V&A: Circ.126—1965

'Sixty three', 'Division' and 'Shape' hand-printed
cotton furnishing fabrics, designed by Shirley
Craven for Hull Traders Ltd
V&A: Circ.121-E—1965

'Merlin' electric clock, plastic case and metal dial.
Case and dial designed by Robert Welch
Associates, mechanism designed by company
design staff at Westclox Ltd

## 1965

Duke of Edinburgh's Prize for Elegant Design:
Auditorium seating, stove-enamelled steel frame
with cast-iron swivel plates and upholstered
plywood back and seat, designed by Peter
Dickinson for Race Contracts Ltd
V&A: Circ.13&A—1966

Hospital wall light, anodized aluminium reflector,
chromium-plated steel arm and cast aluminium
wall-plate, designed by Roger Brockbank for Atlas
Lighting Ltd

'Embassy' silverware, sterling silver, designed
and manufactured by David Mellor for British
embassies
V&A: Circ.674 to 676F—1965

'Legend' furnishing fabric, printed cotton satin,
designed by Alan Reynolds for Edinburgh Weavers
V&A: Circ.541—1963, Circ.26—1966,
T.147:1-3—2009

'Pic' slide rule, polymethyl methacrylate, designed
by Norman Stevenson with company design staff
at A.G. Thornton Ltd
V&A: Circ.23—1966

'Gaylec' convector heater, chrome steel outlet with
polypropylene handles, designed by Bernard Burns
for Carnscot Engineers Ltd
V&A: Circ.18—1966

'Hille Wall Storage System Series 1', particleboard, with a range of veneer and plastic laminate finishes, designed by Alan Turville and John Lewak for S. Hille & Co. Ltd

'Yard-arm' pick-up stick, aluminium with nickel-plated steel grippers sheathed in rubber, and stainless steel mechanism, designed by D.A. Morton for Mabar Manufacturing Co. Ltd
V&A: Circ.19—1966

Range of rag dolls, printed cotton, designed by Joy and Malcolm Wilcox for Sari Fabrics Ltd
V&A: Circ.21:1-4&6—1966

'Arrow-Slim' range of fluorescent light fittings, plastic shades, copper or raffia baffles, designed by Peter Rodd and John Sidney Barnes for Atlas Lighting Ltd
V&A: Circ.17-H—1966

'University' striped blankets and bedspreads for student lodgings, wool, designed by H.W. Rothschild and Primavera Design Group for Primavera (Contracts) Ltd
V&A: Circ.25-B—1966

'Kistna' furnishing fabric, rayon, designed by Nicholas Sekers for West Cumberland Silk Mills Ltd
V&A: Circ.27&A—1966

Electrical ceiling roses and switches, plastic. Shape designed by London and Upjohn, engineering design by GEC for GEC (Installation Equipment) Ltd
V&A: Circ.24—1966

'Mark II' stacking chair, injection-moulded polypropylene shell on metal base with a range of finishes, designed by Robin Day for S. Hille & Co. Ltd
V&A: Circ.15-B—1966

'Meridian One' sanitary suite, vitreous glazed fireclay with acrylic WC seat, designed by Knud Holscher and Alan Tye with Alan H. Adams for Adamsez Ltd
V&A: Circ.16-B—1966, Circ.28 to 33—1966

'G.100' saw, cold-rolled steel blade with polypropylene handle, designed by Brian Asquith for Spear and Jackson Ltd
V&A: Circ.22—1966

'Alveston' cutlery, stainless steel, designed by Robert Welch for Old Hall Tableware Ltd
V&A: Circ.354-F—1965, Circ.20-O—1966

### 1966

Duke of Edinburgh's Prize for Elegant Design: Range of jewellery, precious stones set in 18-carat gold, platinum and white gold, designed by Andrew Grima for H.J. Company Ltd

'Modric' range of architectural ironmongery, anodized aluminium with stainless steel fixings and nylon bushings, designed by Knud Holscher and Alan Tye for G. & S. Allgood Ltd
V&A: Circ.396—1967

'Flexible' chair, laminated beech frame with nylon-coated steel mesh seat and back, and leather arms, with cushions upholstered in a range of fabrics, designed by Nicholas Frewing for Race Furniture Ltd
V&A: Circ.388—1967

'Cantilever' fluorescent desk lamp, anodized aluminium with a steel base, designed by Gerald Abramovitz for Best & Lloyd Ltd
V&A: Circ.392 & 393—1967

'Barbican' hand basin, Ceramant vitreous ceramic, designed by Chamberlin, Powell & Bon with company design staff under Munroe Blair at Twyfords Ltd
V&A: Circ.395—1967

'1108' (mono) and '1111' (stereo) radios, teak-veneered cabinet with anodized aluminium trim and legs, designed by Robin Day and Douglas Jones for Pye of Cambridge Ltd
V&A: Circ.394—1967

'Automatic 1501' washing machine, stove-enamelled steel cabinet with vitreous enamelled lid and aluminium console panel, designed by Industrial Design Unit Ltd with the Home Laundry Engineering Division of AEI-Hotpoint Ltd
V&A: Circ.390—1967

'Quartet Major' display lighting, die-cast aluminium, designed by Robert Heritage for Rotaflex Manufacturing Ltd
V&A: Circ.385 to 387—1967

'Credaplan Individual Quick-Discs' electric hotplates, designed by Creda Design Centre for Simplex Electric Co. Ltd
V&A: Circ.391—1967

**'STC Deltaphone' (marketed as 'GPO Trimphone') telephone for public networks, and 'STC Deltaline' telephone for internal use, ABS plastic bodies and handsets with polycarbonate switching bars and dial finger plates and rubber feet, designed by Martyn Rowlands with STC engineers for Standard Telephones and Cables Ltd**
**V&A: Circ.389—1967, W.65 to 67—2002**

'Hamilton' kitchen and tableware, stoneware with rubber seals and teak lids, designed by D. Tarquin Cole and John Minshaw for Govancroft Potteries Ltd
V&A: Circ.398 to 415—1967

'Thrift' cutlery (also marketed as 'Minim'), stainless steel, designed by David Mellor for the Ministry of Public Building and Works
V&A: Circ.397-D—1967

### 1967

Duke of Edinburgh's Prize for Elegant Design: 'Gas-Flo' gas supply system for domestic use, brass-plated metal with plastic cover-plates, designed by R. David Carter with Malcolm Scott and Ben Wilson, Wales Gas Board engineers, manufactured by Thomas Glover & Co. Ltd for Wales Gas Board
V&A: Circ.503—1968

'Tempest' racing yacht, polyester/glass fibre laminate hull and deck with steel keel, aluminium mast and boom, mahogany beam and coamings and Terylene sails, designed by Ian Proctor for Richardson Boats & Plastics Ltd

Graphic system for directional information road signs, designed by Jock Kinneir and Margaret Calvert, manufactured by various companies for the Ministry of Transport

'Iced Diamond' refrigerators, models 85 and 105, stove-enamelled steel with polyurethane foam insulation and polystyrene liner, designed by Industrial Design Unit Ltd with company design staff at Hotpoint Ltd

'PU Work Station' range of office furniture, aluminium alloy frames with beech doors and drawers, and chipboard side panels and tops finished in linoleum, designed by Planning Unit Ltd and manufactured by D. Meredew Ltd for Interiors International Ltd

'International' range of electric convector radiators, stove-enamelled mild steel with PVC trim and chromium-plated feet, designed by Frank Height and Michael Parr with company design staff at Morphy-Richards
V&A: Circ.505—1968

'Ilfoprint' photo processors, models 951, 1501 and 2001, designed by Kenneth Lamble of the Design Research Unit with company technical staff at Ilford Ltd
V&A: Circ.506—1968

### 1968

Duke of Edinburgh's Prize for Elegant Design: 'Nova' range of tableware, styrene acrylonitrile co-polymer, designed by David Harman Powell for Ekco Plastics Ltd
V&A: Circ.793-E—1968

'Simple Solar' and 'Five' furnishing fabrics, cotton satin and linen cotton union respectively, designed by Shirley Craven for Hull Traders Ltd
V&A: Circ.759 & 760—1967, Circ.791 & 792—1968

'Kompas 1' self-assembly occasional table, laminated melamine and resin-bonded bagasse top and base with a steel stem, designed by Alan Turville for S. Hille & Co. Ltd
V&A: Circ.782—1968

'Those Things' self-assembly children's furniture, polyurethane-coated laminated paper, designed by Peter Murdoch for Perspective Designs Ltd
V&A: Circ.794 to 796—1968, Circ.17 & 18—1970

'Reigate' rocking chair, nylon-coated steel frame with anodized aluminium seat and back supports and upholstered cushions; and 'Coulsdon' coffee table, glass top and steel frame, designed and manufactured by William Plunkett
V&A: Circ.783 & 784—1968

'Sealmaster' door and window seals, heat-treated aluminium alloy and neoprene, designed by Bernard Dixon, E.L. Brooks and R.F. Macdonald for Sealmaster Ltd
V&A: Circ.798-R—1968

'Trimline' ceiling or wall light, polypropylene, designed by Paul Boissevain for Merchant Adventurers Ltd
V&A: Circ.781—1968

**'International' kitchen units, particle board with polyester laminate surfaces, designed by Nigel V. Walters for F. Wrighton & Sons Ltd**

'Silverspan' fluorescent light fittings, aluminium and plastic batten and anodized aluminium attachments. Batten designed by Robert Heritage, attachments designed by Luciano Zucchi for Concord Lighting International Ltd, a Rotaflex (GB) Ltd company
V&A: Circ.780-B—1968

'Clamcleats' rope cleats, nylon, designed by R.J. Emery and Colin R. Cheetham for Clamcleats Ltd
V&A: Circ.797-C—1968

Furnishing fabrics, printed cotton. 'Chevron' designed by Lucienne Day; 'Complex' designed by Barbara Brown; and 'Extension' designed by Haydon Williams for Heal Fabrics Ltd
V&A: Circ.30 & 31—1968, Circ.785 to 790—1968

'Trilateral' poster display unit, steel core and base set in concrete, with galvanized iron and steel structure and plywood or illuminated Perspex poster mount, designed by Ronald Denton for London and Provincial Poster Group Ltd

## 1969

Duke of Edinburgh's Prize for Elegant Design: 'MD2' cash dispenser, heavy-gauge stainless steel fascia, designed by Jack Howe for Chubb & Sons Lock & Safe Co. Ltd

'Larch', 'Rowan', 'Spruce' and 'Aspen' woven upholstery fabrics, wool and viscose backed with acrylic, designed by Bernat Klein for Margo Fabrics Ltd
V&A: Circ.717 to 721–1969

Vymura wall coverings, gravure-printed vinyl. 'Gemini' designed by Susan Faulkner; 'Solitaire' designed by Pat Turnbull; and 'Tempo' designed by Robin Gregson-Brown for ICI Ltd
V&A: Circ.722 to 724–1969

'Polychrome', 'Concentric' and 'Mitre' furnishing fabrics, cotton, designed by Cathryn Netherwood for Heal Fabrics Ltd
V&A: Circ.33–1969, Circ.725 to 727–1969

Restaurant chairs for the QE2, upholstered plywood shell laminated with Formica on an aluminium base, designed by Robert Heritage for Race Furniture Ltd
V&A: Circ.711–1969, Circ.765&A–1969

'BOL1100', 'BOL1150' and 'BOL1050' bollard lights, stove-enamelled aluminium body mounted on a steel tube with glass lens, designed by P.E. Pizzey and H.G. Davies for Frederick Thomas & Co.
V&A: Circ.713–1969

'Quad 303' stereo power amplifier, 'Quad' VHF/FM stereo radio-tuner and 'Quad 33' control unit, aluminium and stove-enamelled steel chassis and covers, designed and manufactured by Acoustical Manufacturing Co. Ltd
V&A: Circ.730-B–1969

'Mercury 33' dead latch, designed by David Carter with company design staff at Yale Locks & Hardware

'Superjet' reading light, polypropylene with anodized aluminium head, designed by Robert Heritage for Concord Lighting International Ltd

'Kangol Reflex' car safety belt, Terylene webbing strap and magnetic buckle in cast aluminium housing, designed and manufactured by Kangol Magnet Ltd
V&A: Circ.715–1969

'Ease-e-load' domestic and general-purpose trolleys, enamelled steel frame and nylon bushings, designed by Harold Martin for Deavin-Irvine Products Ltd
V&A: Circ.728–1969

'Roanrail 2' hospital cubicle curtain track, anodized aluminium rail with nylon runners and ABS plastic mouldings, designed by Bernard Burns for Roanoid Ltd
V&A: Circ.712–1969

'Big Screen' display and exhibition units, hessian-covered soft board panels in hardwood frames with chromium-plated poles, designed by Brian C. Bannister for Marler Haley (Barnet) Ltd

## 1970

Duke of Edinburgh's Prize for Elegant Design: 'Fish' and 'Bird' bath toys, 'Gyrosphere', 'Mosaic', 'Playplax' and 'Little Men' toys, polystyrene and ABS plastic, designed by Patrick Rylands for Trendon Ltd
V&A: Misc.41 to 46–1970, Circ.348 to 353–1970

'Star' range of mobile radio-telephones, steel or polycarbonate cases with chromed aluminium control panels, and melamine and ABS plastic handles and buttons, designed by Kenneth Grange with company design staff at Standard Telephones & Cables Ltd

'Opella 500 series' taps, injection-moulded acetal co-polymer with acrylic heads, designed by Martyn Rowlands with company design staff at IMI Developments Ltd
V&A: Circ.354 to 357–1970

**'Neptune', 'Mars', 'Vulcan', 'Apollo', 'Aurora' and 'Diana' lamps, ceramic and opal glass, designed by Martin Hunt and James Kirkwood; ceramic ash bowls designed by Helena Uglow for JRM Design Sales Ltd**
**V&A: Circ.75 to 81–1977**

'Knockdown' storage system, hardboard panels with galvanized steel or polished aluminium uprights and plastic-covered steel hanging rails, designed by Henry Kewley and P.R. Kilbey for Kewlox Ltd

'Savannah' solid-fuel heating unit, steel with cast-iron components and stove-enamelled cast aluminium doors, designed by Brian Asquith with company design staff at Redfyre Ltd

'Hedway' signage system, stainless steel, designed by Knud Holscher and Alan Tye for Syncronol Industries Ltd

Disposable cutlery, styrene acrylonitrile co-polymer, designed by David Harman Powell for Ekco Plastics Ltd
V&A: Circ.334 to 337–1970

Dining chairs and tables, chromed steel frames with glass tops, rubber supports and PVC or leather upholstery, designed by Ray Exton and Peter Wigglesworth for Plush Kicker Ltd

'Muraweave' collection of wall coverings, jute laminated to wallpaper, designed by Mary Abbott for Boyle & Son Ltd
V&A: Circ.345 to 347–1970

'Red Herring', 'Robert Frieze', 'Minaret', 'Rabat', 'Inferno Frieze', 'Jonas Cord', 'Queen's Knight', 'Fitzherbert' and 'Koh-I-Nor' wallpapers, hand-printed paper, designed by Antony Little for Osborne & Little Ltd
V&A: Circ.338 to 344–1970, E.856 & 858–1978

'Hebridean' range of furnishing fabrics, wool blended with cotton, nylon or alpaca, designed by William Robertson and Peter Simpson for Donald Bros Ltd
V&A: Circ.264 to 273–1970

'Spiral' and 'Automation' furnishing fabrics, printed cotton, designed by Barbara Brown for Heal Fabrics Ltd
V&A: Circ.777 & 784–1969, Circ.274 to 279–1970, T.279–1990, T.288:1-3–1999

'Hexagon', 'Crossbridge', 'Daisytile', 'Nico', 'Montpelier', 'Large Quatrefoil', 'Maltese Cross' and 'Wentworth' – 'Kensington' range of Brussels carpets, wool and nylon, designed by David Hicks with company designers Colin Royle and John Palmer at John Crossley & Sons Ltd
V&A: T.348-G–1988

## 1971

Duke of Edinburgh's Prize for Elegant Design: 'Teltron' range of atomic physics teaching equipment, wood and glass cases on aluminium alloy plinths with cathode tubes, designed by Derek Power and Dennis Beard with Noel Haring Associates for Teltron Ltd
V&A: Circ.455-C–1971

'Mariner' nautical instruments, barometer, clock, and thermometer/hygrometer, anodized aluminium casings with acrylic faces, polystyrene back panels and stainless steel wall mount brackets, designed by Kenneth Grange. Manufactured by Taylor Instruments Companies (Europe) Ltd

Photographic darkroom equipment range, polystyrene, designed by Eric Taylor for Paterson Products Ltd
V&A: Circ.253 to 259–1971

'Impregnable' padlocks, laminated steel body, copper brazed and finished in nickel chrome, with chrome-plated hardened steel shackle, designed and manufactured by Ingersoll Locks Ltd
V&A: Circ.260 & 261–1971

'Globoot' children's waterproof boots, PVC plastisol uppers and soles with removable sock, designed by Globoot Footwear for Plastic Coatings Ltd
V&A: Circ.250 to 252–1971, TN.283 & 284–2011

'Powerflood' miniature floodlamp, aluminium with tungsten halogen lamp, designed by Robert Heritage with company design staff at Concord Lighting International
V&A: Circ.85–1973

Back-projection slide preview screen, textured polystyrene with a rear-silvered mirror, designed by Martyn Rowlands for Boots Pure Drug Co. Ltd

'Avenger 16' powerboat, glass-reinforced plastic deck and hull, designed by Don Shead for Avenger Boat Co. Ltd

## 1972

Duke of Edinburgh's Prize for Elegant Design: Range of kitchen and table wares, glass, designed by Frank Thrower for Dartington Glass Ltd

Duke of Edinburgh's Prize for Elegant Design: Geological or polarizing triple objective microscope, ABS plastic case, designed by Dr John McArthur, manufactured by Scientific Optics Ltd for the Open University

'Interchangeable' jewellery range, gold with enamel and semi-precious stones, designed and made by Wendy Ramshaw
V&A: M.169–1976, M.34-D–1982

Kinetic effect lighting system, screens in punched metal, textured glass and plain glass, designed and manufactured by Concord Lighting International Ltd
V&A: Circ.459, 461-M, 462, 463 & 465-E–1973

**Wall and floor tiles, hand-glazed ceramics, designed by Sally Anderson for Sally Anderson (Ceramics) Ltd**
**V&A: Circ.430 to 442–1973**

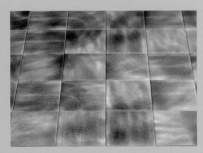

'Baby Belling' boiling table and oven/grill unit, designed and manufactured by Belling & Co. Ltd

Children's playground equipment, metal, wood and tyres, designed and manufactured by SMP (Landscapes) Ltd

Bonded shaving system, black glass-filled polycarbonate handle with aluminium backing, stainless steel blade, ABS plastic cap and guard and polysulfone plastic latch and ejector, designed and manufactured by Wilkinson Sword Ltd

'Island Lace' furnishing fabric, machine lace, designed by Peter Simpson and manufactured by Darvel Textiles Ltd for Donald Bros Ltd
V&A: Circ.451 to 453–1973

'DTLV 20' spotlight, aluminium reflector and tungsten halogen lamp. From the 'Atlas Hi-Spot' range designed and manufactured by Thorn Lighting Ltd
V&A: Circ.455–1973

Post franking machine, designed by H.A. Nieboer for Roneo-Neopost Ltd
V&A: Circ.454–1973

'Variset' range of hat and coat hooks, aluminium, designed by Kenneth Grange for A.J. Binns Ltd
V&A: Circ.444 to 450–1973

'Sapphire' range of electrical tools, glass-reinforced plastic casings and plastic shrouds, designed and manufactured by Wolf Electric Tools Ltd
V&A: Circ.457 & 458–1973

Range of stretch upholstery fabrics, wool, designed by Gordon Cant for Abbotsford Fabrics
V&A: Circ.422 to 429–1973

## 1973

Duke of Edinburgh's Prize for Elegant Design: Picture framing system, acrylic and extruded aluminium with polystyrene-filled aluminium internal frame, designed by George Robins for Design Animations Ltd

**'Lytespan 7' extruded aluminium lighting track, and 'Eurospot' and 'Pan Parabolic' lights, designed by Robert Heritage with company designers at Concord Lighting International Ltd**
**V&A: Circ.464–1973, Circ.84 & 86 to 89–1977, TN.285 & 286–2011**

'Callbuoy series 14A' distress radio-telephone, glass-reinforced plastic box with ABS plastic cap and silicone rubber buttons, designed and manufactured by LRW Electronics Ltd
V&A: Circ.467–1973

'Wharfedale Isodynamic' headphones, ABS plastic moulded shell and stainless steel headband, designed by Oliver Hill with the Rank Radio Industrial Design Unit for Rank Radio International Ltd
V&A: Circ.466–1973

'OlympiCastor' furniture castors, metal wheel with nylon or polyurethane tyre, designed and manufactured by Archibald Kenrick & Sons Ltd
V&A: Circ.471 to 475–1973

'Sinclair Executive' electronic calculator, with LED screen, designed and manufactured by Sinclair Radionics Ltd

'Wilton Stripe' carpet collection, wool and nylon, designed and manufactured by Brintons Ltd
V&A: Circ.477 to 485–1973

'Workmate Mark 2' workbench, metal frame and wooden work-surfaces, designed by Ron Hickman for Black & Decker Ltd
V&A: Circ.469–1973

'Bardolino', 'Bida', 'Bonito' and 'Baccarini' upholstery fabrics, woven wool, cotton and nylon, designed and manufactured by Sekers Fabrics Ltd
V&A: Circ.486–1973, Circ.489 to 493A–1973

Photographic enlarger, ABS plastic baseboard surfaced with metal plate and polycarbonate main body, designed by Donald Paterson and Eric Taylor for Paterson Products Ltd
V&A: Circ.470–1973

Range of extruded plastic garden netting, polypropylene and polyethylene, designed by Brian Mercer for Netlon Ltd
V&A: Circ.476-P–1973

'Village Churches' stamps, first day cover and presentation pack, printed paper, designed by Ronald Maddox for the Post Office
V&A: Circ.497&A–1973

## 1974

'Hipak' range of mercury vapour light fittings for high industrial buildings and public areas, aluminium with zinc-plated, stove-enamelled steel outer frame, designed by Colin Dipper for Thorn Lighting Ltd
V&A: Circ.90-B–1977

'Bino Compass' miniature long-range bearing compass, plastic with glass-reinforced noryl collar, designed by Michael Dupree with company design staff at Offshore Instruments Ltd
V&A: Circ.91–1977

'Sorbo-Ski' artificial ski slope, alkathene ethylene/vinyl acetate co-polymer, designed by John Blandford Jupe and Roy L. Manns for Summer Ski Ltd

'700 range' of chairs and tables, steel with vitreous-enamelled tabletops and PVC and polyether cushions, designed by David Mellor for Abacus Municipal Ltd
V&A: Circ.119 & 120–1977

'One Eleven' and 'Two Eleven' ranges of wall coverings, wool laminated on to hessian with foam backing, designed by Jean-Pierre Teroy for Jean-Pierre Teroy Décor Ltd
V&A: Circ.92-X–1977

'AC1' and 'AP1' pre-amplifier and power amplifier audio units, matt black aluminium and Perspex, designed by Robert Stuart and Allen Boothroyd for Lecson Audio Ltd
V&A: Circ.70&A–1977

'Input' range of heavy-duty containers, ABS plastic, designed by Conran Associates for Crayonne Ltd
V&A: Circ.99 to 116–1977

'Blazer', 'Honeycomb' and 'Crockfords' wall and floor tiles, hand-decorated glazed ceramic, designed by Tarquin Cole for Rye Tiles
V&A: C.188 to 194 & 197–1984

'Aga A50' wall-recessed gas boiler, aluminium-coated mild steel with stove-enamelled steel casing, designed and manufactured by Agaheat Appliances

'4824 Auto-Jet 12' and '4834 Super-Jet 12' dishwashers, designed by Paul Moss and Cedric Mastin for Hoover Ltd
V&A: TN.287–2011

## 1975

Duke of Edinburgh's Prize for Elegant Design: 'Bullet' racing dinghy, aluminium hull, designed by Peter Milne for Chippendale & Milne Ltd

'Fabric Printing Kit', 'Candlemaking Tub', 'Colour in the Round', 'Busy Board' and 'Rainy Day Colouring Kit' children's craft kits, various art materials in cardboard and plastic packaging, designed by Larking Stratton & May for Reeves & Sons Ltd
V&A: Circ.94 to 98–1977

'Philips MA SOX' street lighting lantern range, glass-reinforced plastic canopy and acrylic refractor bowl, designed by A. Butowsky and B. Rogers for Philips Electrical Ltd (Lighting Division)

'Contrast' Lancaster tableware, vitrified ceramic, designed by Martin Hunt for Hornsea Pottery Co. Ltd
V&A: Circ.48 to 67–1977, Circ.123–1977

'Junior Kwiktower' and 'Multicover' scaffolding system, tubular steel with wood platforms and rubber feet, designed and manufactured by Kwikform Ltd

Periodical display rack and book rest, stove-enamelled mild steel, designed by John Marshall for Marico Furniture Ltd
V&A: Circ.72 to 74–1977

'Accelerator' compost bins, PVC, designed by Clifford Wilson for Rotocrop Ltd
V&A: Circ.82:1-38–1977

**'Brix' curtain fabric, hand-printed wool, designed by Anna Caldwell for Margo International Fabrics**
**V&A: Circ.117 & 118–1977**

Air safety blowgun with Venturi attachment, nylon with brass nozzle, designed by Geoffrey E. Speyer for Taylor & Osborne Ltd
V&A: Circ.93&A–1977

'Ilfospeed 4250 Dryer', aluminium case with stainless steel fascia, neoprene rollers and ABS components, designed by John Wickham of Bell-Wickham Associates with company design staff at Ilford Ltd
V&A: Circ.71–1977

## 1976

Duke of Edinburgh's Prize for Elegant Design: 'Blatchford' modular prosthesis, designed by Brian Blatchford for Charles A. Blatchford & Sons Ltd

'Clipstor' storage system, aluminium rails with glass-filled nylon brackets and nylon and ABS plastic attachments, designed by Height & Guille with company design staff at Black & Decker Ltd
V&A: Circ.16–1977

'Autohelm' and 'Autohelm Plus' electronic wind vane boat steering systems, designed by Derek Fawcett for Nautech Ltd
V&A: Circ.124–1977

'Studio One' range of Vymura wall coverings, screen-printed vinyl, designed by Sue Faulkner for ICI Ltd (Paints Division)
V&A: Circ.17–1977, E.1034 to 1124–1979

'Quad 405 Power Amplifier', aluminium casing, designed and manufactured by The Acoustical Manufacturing Co. Ltd
V&A: Circ.15–1977

'Molyneux Gully' trapped drainage gully with rodding access, uPVC, designed by Roy Letts and George Molyneux for G. Molyneux (Products) Ltd
V&A: Circ.21–1977

Colour-coordinated range of fire extinguishers, designed and manufactured by Chubb Fire & Security Ltd
V&A: Circ.23–1977

'Waltham' kitchen units, particle-board with plastic laminate worktops, doors finished in wood veneer or metallic or polyester laminate, with aluminium trim, designed by Nigel V. Walters for Wrighton International Furniture
V&A: Circ.30 & 31–1977

**'Good Companions' range of Axminster carpets and rugs, wool, designed by David Bartle and manufactured by Broadloom Carpets Ltd**
**V&A: Circ.24 to 29–1977**

'Peacock', 'Plumage', 'Rainstorm', 'Multiwave', 'Tiderace', 'Willow', 'Wych Elm' and 'Meadow Grass' – 'One Step On' range of wall tiles, ceramic with designs applied as layers of glaze, designed by Sally Anderson for Sally Anderson (Ceramics) Ltd
V&A: Circ.32 to 39–1977

## 1977

Duke of Edinburgh's Prize for Elegant Design: Mardrive linear transporter, designed by George Carroll for The Marine Engineering Co. (Stockport)

'Concept' tableware, vitrified ceramic, designed by Martin Hunt and Colin Bentley Rawson for Hornsea Pottery Co. Ltd
V&A: C.207-K–1977, C.9-E–1990

'Chinese Ivory' and 'Chinese Black' cutlery, stainless steel and acetal resin, designed and manufactured by David Mellor
V&A: M.3-E–1978

'Sovereign' calculator, chrome-finished steel case and LED display, designed by John Pemberton, John Holland and Victor Thomas for Sinclair Radionics Ltd
V&A: M.17–1991

Airfield lighting equipment, with tungsten halogen lamps, designed by Graham Willmott with company designers Ron Gosling, David Bridgers and Brian Titmarsh at Thorn Lighting Ltd
V&A: TN.288–2011

'Tubetrack 7' lighting system, designed by Robert Heritage and Luciano Zucchi for Concord Lighting International Ltd

'Countdown CD1' digital clock, ABS plastic case, designed by John Ryan for House of Carmen Ltd
V&A: W.72–1978

'Topper' sailing dinghy, injection-moulded polypropylene, designed by Ian Proctor for J.V. Dunhill Boats Ltd

'Format O-Series' door handles and accessories, aluminium, designed by Murdoch & Gibbs for James Gibbons Ltd

## 1978

Duke of Edinburgh's Prize for Elegant Design: 'Micro 2000' digital electronic micrometer, designed by John Fisher of Patscentre International for Moore & Wright (Sheffield) Ltd

'Micro' folding bicycle, enamelled metal frame and epoxy handlebars, controls, brakes and gears, designed by Peter Radnall for Micro Cycles Ltd

'SME Series III' precision pick-up arm, nitrogen-hardened titanium and carbon fibre reinforced plastics, designed by Alastair Robertson-Aikman and William R. Edey for SME Ltd

'Microvision' pocket television, steel case and plastic buttons, designed by John Pemberton and company designers at Sinclair Radionics Ltd
V&A: TN.261–2011

## 1979

Duke of Edinburgh's Prize for Elegant Design: 'Sea Truck' briefcase and naval design equipment, designed by Jeremy Fry of Bill Moggridge Associates for Rotork Marine Ltd

'Ducktiles' interlocking non-slip flooring, polypropylene with high-friction treads, designed by Peter Mellor of Ferodo and Peter Mead of British Industrial Plastics for Ferodo

'Tinker Tramp' inflatable dinghy, rubber with plywood floor, aluminium mast and wooden dagger board and rudder, designed by Fred Benyon-Tinker for J.M. Henshaw (Marine) Ltd

'Paterson' photographic darkroom equipment, polystyrene, polypropylene and stainless steel, designed by Eric Taylor for Paterson Products

'Tensabarrier', nylon-coated mild steel poles and bases with polyester webbing, designed by David Hodge of David Hodge Associates for the British Airports Authority, manufactured by Tensator

'Azurene' vases, hand-blown glass with silver and gold leaf, designed after an original idea by William Walker, made by Isle of Wight Studio Glass
V&A: C.144 to 147–1979

## 1980

Duke of Edinburgh's Prize for Elegant Design: 'Groundsat', compact VHF (FM) transceiver system, aluminium alloy case, designed and manufactured by Plessey Avionics & Communications

'Tigh' and 'Orlem' contract upholstery fabric collections, wool, designed by A.C. Driver, F.A. Donnelly and W. Wallace for Donald Brothers Ltd

'Stowaway' folding dinghy, aluminium frame with woven polyester-reinforced PVC skin, PVC underside and polythene seat filled with expanded polystyrene, designed by Jean François Raymond for Vango (Scotland) Ltd

'Praddel' single-handed paddle, polypropylene, designed by Ian Proctor for Ian Proctor Design

'Amstad' range of perch seating, polypropylene seats on steel pivot rods, designed by David Goodwin, Peter Wheeler and Andrew Smyth for Amstad Systems Ltd

'Britax' yachting harness, Terylene webbing with stainless steel buckle and attachments, designed by Peter Hankey and R.T. Hunt for Britax-Excelsior Ltd

'Corinthian' light switches, urea-formaldehyde, designed by E.J. Butcher and J.A. Vale for Crabtree Electrical Industries Ltd

'Bramah BP17' high-security padlock, stainless steel, designed by R.K. Burrough for Bramah Security Equipment Ltd

## 1981

Duke of Edinburgh's Prize for Elegant Design: 'Mini Metro' car, designed by Raymond Bates, Mark Snowdon and David Bache for British Leyland Cars Ltd

'Mark II' roller-skate chassis, aluminium alloy with polyurethane wheels, designed by Bryan Eccles for Freewheeler Leisure Products Ltd

'The Terence Piper Personalized Refreshment Service PRS67' drinks machine, designed by Terence Piper and company design staff with Kenneth Grange for VGL Industries Ltd

'Max 150G' tennis racket, carbon fibre-reinforced nylon frame filled with polyurethane, designed and manufactured by Dunlop Sports Co. Ltd

'Gibb 75TA' self-tailing winch, black anodized aluminium with Delrin acetal resin bearing, designed by David Tyler for M.S. Gibb Ltd

'Hercules System 190', yacht instrumentation system, plastic casing and LCD displays, designed and manufactured by Brookes & Gatehouse Ltd

'Boulevard' range of street furniture, concrete with coarse aggregate, designed by David Hodge of Fisher Hodge Ltd, manufactured by Mono Concrete Ltd for the British Airports Authority

'Lo-Kata 5' radio compass, designed by Cosmo Little, Richard Wigram and Tom Tivendale for Magnetic Components Ltd

## 1982

Duke of Edinburgh's Prize for Elegant Design: Advanced Technology Flight Simulator with central 32-bit computer, designed and manufactured by Rediffusion Simulation Ltd

'Homer 5' marine radio receiver, glass-filled ABS and polycarbonate casing, designed and manufactured by Brookes & Gatehouse Ltd

'Meridian' modular amplifier system, designed by Allen Boothroyd and Robin Stuart for Boothroyd Stuart Ltd

'DDH' golf ball, wound thread with a polymer blend casing, designed by R.C. Haines and M. Shaw for Dunlop Sports Co. Ltd

'Supporto' range of office chairs, aluminium shell with epoxy resin or nylon finish and upholstered seat and back, designed by Fred Scott for Hille International Ltd
V&A: W.2 to 5–1981

'Mark IV' single racing scull, Kevlar and carbon fibre shell with English ash shoulders, cedar deck and spruce frame, designed by G.A.S. Locke and S.J. Adcock for Glyn Locke (Racing Shells) Ltd

'Red Handflare Mark 6' and 'Handsmoke Mark 2' marine distress flares, designed by Michael Cunnell, Dave Robinson, Nigel Joslin and Malcolm Youd for Pains-Wessex Ltd

'Darkroom Safelight', with translucent polycarbonate cover, and 'E300' digital thermometer, stainless steel with ABS plastic handle, designed by Eric Taylor for Paterson Products Ltd

**'ZX81' personal computer, with plastic case and integrated membrane keyboard, designed by Rick Dickinson, manufactured by Timex Corporation for Sinclair Research Ltd**

'Ebony' tableware, glazed stoneware with laminated wood handles, designed by Colin Bentley Rawson and Michael Walker with Martin Hunt of Queensberry Hunt for Hornsea Pottery Co. Ltd
V&A: C.271-C–1986

'Liquid Geometry' puzzle toy, acrylic container filled with water, designed by Marcus Smith, Richard Loncraine, Michael Connell and Peter Broxton for Loncraine Broxton & Partners

Jigsaw puzzles, mahogany-cored plywood, designed and made by George Luck

Range of cards and wrapping paper, printed paper and card, designed by Farhana Khan and Peter Colman for Farhana Designs

Greetings cards, printed card, designed by Sara Lynn and Andrew Jarvis for Two-Can Design

## 1983

Duke of Edinburgh's Prize for Elegant Design: 'Dandy clip' fastener, nylon, designed by Peter Huxtable, D.J.H. Birt and C. Aycliffe for Wonderclip Ltd

Duke of Edinburgh's Prize for Elegant Design: 'Westland 30 series' helicopter, with twin Rolls Royce Gem 60 engines, designed and manufactured by Westland Helicopters Ltd

'Multiview' spirit level, injection-moulded plastic, designed by J.S. Willetts, D.F. Poole and E.P. Arch for Rabone Chesterman Ltd

'Quadmatic Pack' electronic flash generator, designed by Ken Bowen, Peter Louden, Stan Phillips and John Allwright for Bowens Sales & Service Ltd

'Dragon Fly 60' fly fishing reel, carbon fibre, designed by Keith Duffelen for British Fly Reels Ltd

'Yuki Collection' travel goods, leather, designed by Yuki for Papworth Industries

'Nettle', 'Waterfall', 'Privet', 'Hawthorn', 'Willow Herb', 'Rowan', 'Swallow', 'Peacock', 'Pinion' and 'Alhambra' – 'Midsummer' range, hand-decorated ceramic, designed by Sally Anderson for Sally Anderson (Ceramics) Ltd

'New Wave' wallpapers and printed fabrics, designed by Geoff Pearce, Ian Smith, Don Stewart, Janet Wrench and Maddy Kardesz for House of Mayfair

Greeting cards, wrapping paper, gift tags and bags, printed card, paper and plastic, designed by Emmanuel Ekizoglou and Erofili Kazazis for Millimetre Ltd

'Mindbender' puzzles, Perspex boxes with perforated plastic dividers and plastic balls, designed by Marcus Smith, Richard Loncraine, Michael Connell and Peter Broxton for Loncraine Broxton & Partners Ltd

## 1984

**Duke of Edinburgh's Prize for Elegant Design: 'Romany', 'Spice Route', 'Havana', 'Kasbah', 'Côte d'Azur' and 'Water Meadow' – 'Six Views' range of furnishing fabrics, printed cotton, designed by Susan Collier, Sarah Campbell, Rosemary Barber and Peter Dalla Costa for Collier Campbell Ltd
V&A: T.183 to 187–1984**

'Triangle' range of wire-bound notebooks, designed by Robert and Mario Budwig for Triangle Design

'Tran-Sit' public seating, enamelled steel, designed by Rodney Kinsman and Peter Glynn Smith for OMK Design Ltd

'Guideline 90' pedestrian barrier system, designed by B.C. Bannister and D. Seeley for Marler Haley ExpoSystems Ltd

'Travelaid' range of castors, plastic, designed by R.J. Spencer, A. Gray, J.R. Heathcock and S.T. Screen for British Castors Ltd

'Durabeam' torch, acetal ratchet and internal section with ABS plastic casing, designed by R.J. Winstone, A. Forman and P.J. Pope with J. Drane of BIB Design Consultants for Duracell UK

'Programme 2' office furniture system, steel frames with black melamine panels and wood veneer tops, designed by John Sayer and Nicki Theokritoff for Lucas Furniture Systems Ltd

'STC Executel' business telephone exchange/reception unit, designed by Robert Cross for STC Telecommunications Ltd

'Kitchen Devils' professional kitchen knives, high carbon steel blades and glass-filled polypropylene handles, designed by Robert Welch for Kitchen Devils Ltd

'Orbital Colour Print Processor and Power Drive' photographic processing equipment, polycarbonate, designed by Eric Taylor for Paterson Products Ltd

## 1985

**'Polydron 3D' geometric construction toy, ABS plastic, designed by Edward and Ronan Harvey for Polydron Ltd**

'Nickerson Turfmaster 360' mower, with three cutting cylinders and 12-horsepower engine, designed by F.M. Templeton, G.A. Templeton and W.L. Thompson for Nickerson Turfmaster Ltd

Lightweight garden shears and notched shears, PTFE-coated chromed steel blades and nylon handles, designed by Alan Pittaway and C.R. Harrison for Wilkinson Sword Ltd

## 1986

Duke of Edinburgh's Prize for Elegant Design: 'Patchwork Sampler' knitwear collection and 'Knitkits' craft kits, designed by Patricia Roberts for Patricia Roberts Knitting

'Annelise', 'Marianne', 'Susanna' and 'Sylvie' pleated furnishing fabrics, designed by Fiona Greenwood for Fox & Floor

'Card Human Skeleton' educational toy, printed card, designed by Richard Miller for Fisher-Miller Ltd

'Design Concept' range of carpet tiles, Timbrelle nylon fabric, designed by Bill Naysmith for Stoddard Carpets

'Topsy' litter bin, polyethylene with galvanized steel liner, designed by Eric Palmer for Glasdon Ltd

'Lotus' and 'Combat' cubicles, designed by David Goodwin Design for Thrislington Sales Ltd

'Vigil RM Radar' navigational system for small boats, designed by Derek Roberts for Mars Electronics (Marine Systems Division)

## 1987

'Sirius' and 'Stippleglaze' ranges of fabrics and wallpapers, various materials, designed and manufactured by Osborne & Little

'New Classics' knitwear collection, wool, designed and made by Sarah Dallas

## 1988

'Fragments' and 'Abstracts' ranges of rugs, wool, designed by Fay Morgan and Roger Oates

'Ergo' hip flask, pewter, designed by Chris Middleton for Troika

'Spirals' jewellery, Formica, designed and made by Louise Slater

'DG1' guitar synthesizer, plastic case and stainless steel strings, designed and manufactured by Stepp Digital Guitars

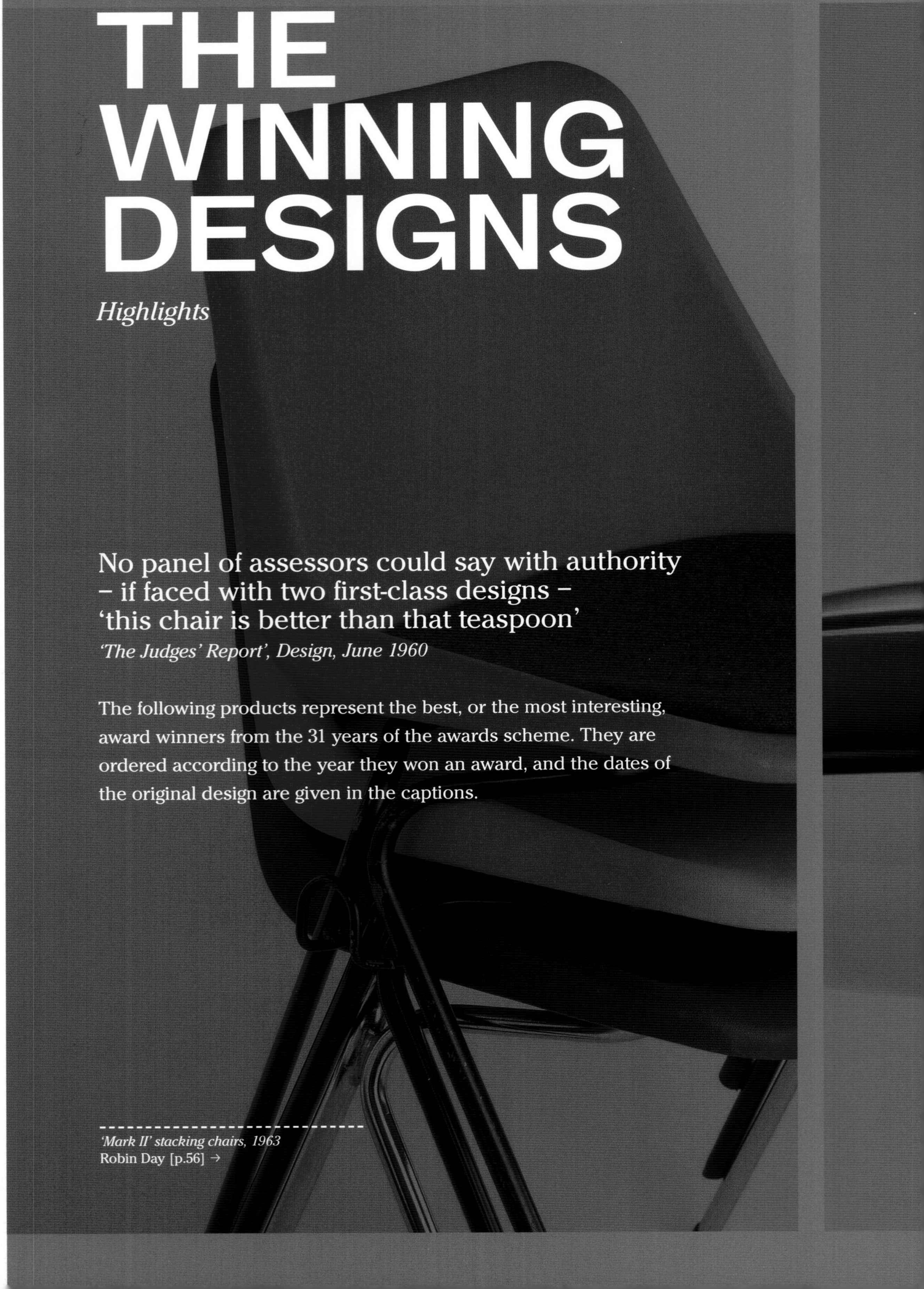

# THE WINNING DESIGNS

*Highlights*

No panel of assessors could say with authority
– if faced with two first-class designs –
'this chair is better than that teaspoon'
*'The Judges' Report', Design, June 1960*

The following products represent the best, or the most interesting, award winners from the 31 years of the awards scheme. They are ordered according to the year they won an award, and the dates of the original design are given in the captions.

----------------------------

*'Mark II' stacking chairs, 1963*
Robin Day [p.56] →

*'Ellipse' pendant light fitting, 1959*
Paul Boissevain [p.41] →

*'Spiral' furnishing fabric, 1969*
Barbara Brown [p.74] →

# *1957* Pride

*'Pride' cutlery*
Designed by David Mellor
for Walker & Hall Ltd, 1953

# *1957* Melmex

*Cup and saucer*
From the 'Melmex' range
of tableware designed by
A.H. Woodfull and John D. Vale
of the Product Design Service,
British Industrial Plastics Ltd;
manufactured by Streetly
Manufacturing Co. for
W.R. Midwinter Ltd, 1957

# *1957* CS17

*'CS17' television*
Cabinet and stand designed by Robin
Day, circuit designed by J.E. Cope for
Pye Ltd, 1957

# *1957* Flamingo

*'Flamingo' furnishing fabric*
Designed by Tibor Reich for Tibor Ltd, 1957

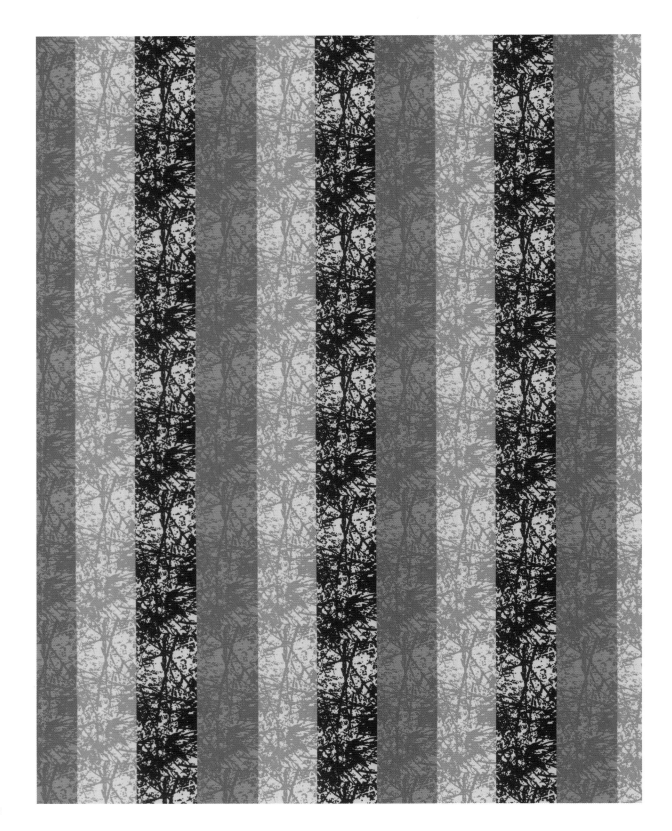

# *1958* Taperback

*'Taperback' occasional chair*
Designed by John Neville Stafford for Stafford
Furniture Ltd, 1956

Award-Winning British Design

1957 – 1988

# *1958* Phantom Rose

*'Phantom Rose' wallpaper*
From the 'Palladio 2' range, designed
by Audrey Levy for The Wall Paper
Manufacturers Ltd, 1958

# *1958* Satina

*'Satina' pendant light fitting*
Designed by Nigel Chapman, manufactured
by Hailwood & Ackroyd for AEI Lamp
& Lighting Co., 1958

# *1958* Conference

*Vegetable tureen*
From the 'Conference' range
of tableware, pattern designed
by Pat Albeck, 'Metro' shape
designed by Tom Arnold for
Ridgway Potteries Ltd, 1958

# *1958* Old Hall

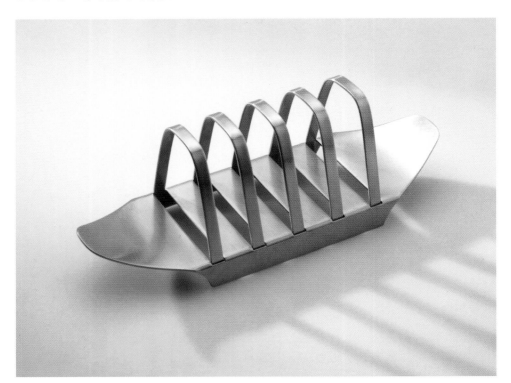

*'Old Hall' toast rack*
Designed by Robert Welch
for J. & J. Wiggin Ltd, 1956

## *1958* Hamilton

*'Hamilton' sideboard*
Dining room set at the CoID 'Living in Britain'
stand, designed by Helen Challen for the 1958
Earls Court Furniture Exhibition, including
the award-winning 'Hamilton' sideboard (left),
designed by Robert Heritage for Archie Shine Ltd

# *1958* Adam

*'Adam' furnishing fabric*
Designed by Keith Vaughan
for Edinburgh Weavers, 1958

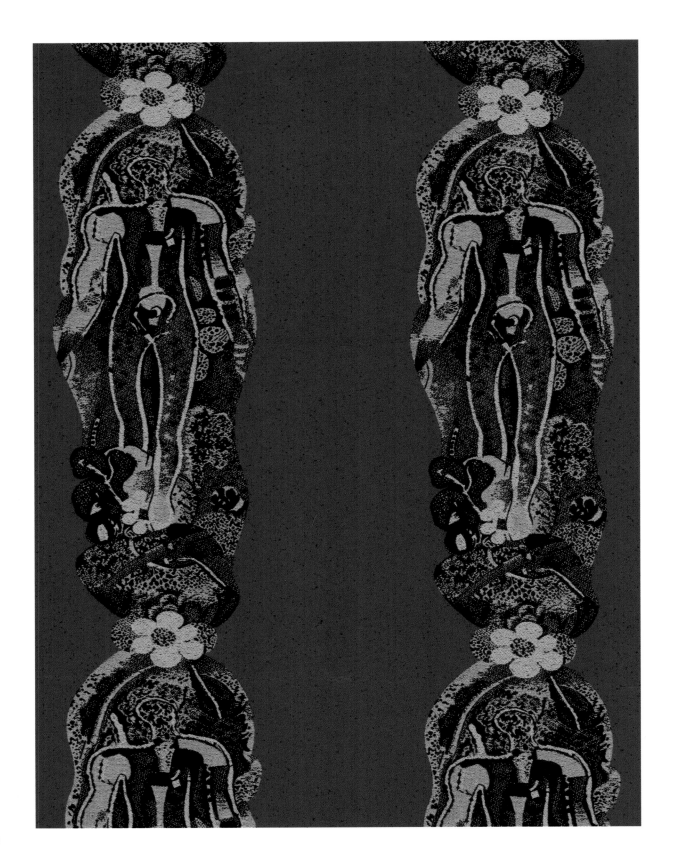

## Furniture

The dominant furniture style in the early years of the awards had its origins in the 1951 Festival of Britain. Known as the Contemporary or Festival style, it was characterized by elegant, economical forms in modern materials and light colours, with details suggestive of atomic structures. Its foremost exponent was furniture designer Ernest Race, who had designed chairs for the Southbank terraces during the Festival.

During the 1960s the emphasis shifted towards more ephemeral design and a 'Pop' aesthetic that favoured such materials as plastics and cardboard. Robin Day's 'Mark II' chair (popularly known as the 'Polyprop') was the first piece of furniture to be made using injection-moulded polypropylene, an inexpensive plastic that was easy to mass produce, as well as being durable, lightweight and flexible. The chair was hugely successful and sold millions around the world. Flat-pack furniture also became increasingly popular as it saved money for manufacturers and consumers. For the first time, furniture was becoming cheap and temporary — young buyers wanted to keep up with the latest fashions, not invest in an heirloom.

*'Cormorant' folding outdoor chair, 1961*
Ernest Race [p.47] →

*'Mark II' stacking chairs, 1963*
Robin Day [p.56] →

## Textiles

Textile manufacturing is a traditional British strength, and several large companies produced award-winning designs. A particularly innovative firm was Edinburgh Weavers, whose art director, Alastair Morton, commissioned ambitious designs from leading artists such as Keith Vaughan and Alan Reynolds. The resulting textiles often had very large-scale patterns, and were favoured by architects for lofty modern interiors. The retailer Heal's focused on finding and nurturing design talent. Tom Worthington, the managing director from 1948 to 1971, sought out gifted young designers in art schools, as well as employing a stable of established names such as Lucienne Day and Barbara Brown.

In the 1960s, 'Pop' designs began to dominate in textiles as elsewhere. Under the art direction of designer Shirley Craven, Hull Traders came to specialize in hand screen-printed fabrics with bright, fashionable designs. As well as commissioning leading designers and artists to design for the company, Craven herself produced more than 40 patterns for Hull Traders in the 1960s and '70s.

Many British designers found their textiles were in demand from international fashion houses. For example, Bernat Klein established a business in the Scottish Borders in 1952 that made vibrantly coloured and textured tweeds, such as the award-winning 'Aspen', and his clients in the 1960s included Chanel, Dior and Balenciaga.

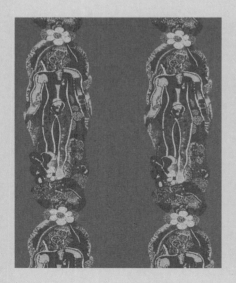

*'Adam' furnishing fabric, 1958*
Keith Vaughan [p.32] →

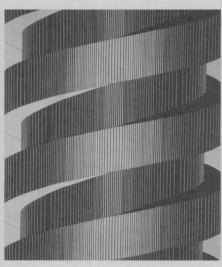

*'Spiral' furnishing fabric, 1969*
Barbara Brown [p.74] →

## Wallpapers and Tiles

Award-winning wallpapers ranged from sophisticated hand screen-printed designs to bold styles made for the fashion-conscious mass market. The 'Palladio' series of wallpaper collections produced by The Wall Paper Manufacturers was aimed at architects and interior designers. Its patterns often had ambitiously large repeats and picked up key trends, including the illustrative and Mediterranean-inspired looks popular in the 1950s, and the more graphic op-art fashions of the 1960s. The majority of award-winning wallpapers came from 'Palladio' collections.

In contrast the Paints Division of chemical manufacturer Imperial Chemical Industries (ICI), the largest manufacturing company in the British Empire, achieved an award for its Vymura wall coverings for the mass market. A producer of domestic and industrial paints, PVC sheeting and coated fabrics, ICI was well-positioned to develop these innovative vinyl-coated wall coverings, which required great technical expertise to overcome problems of shrinkage and poor printing registration; ICI also had to develop its own inks to achieve the necessary opacity for printing on to the plastic surface.

Great diversity in style could also be found among the winning tile designs, from bright 'Pop' patterns in the 1960s to nature-inspired motifs in the 1970s. Some of the most interesting award winners were handmade on a relatively small scale. For example, potter Sally Anderson was running a small workshop in the new town of Harlow when in 1970 she received her first major commission to make tiles for an international hotel in London. This led her to found Sally Anderson (Ceramics) Ltd, which specialized in hand-painted tiles with sophisticated glaze effects.

'Kelpie' wallpaper, 1976
Sue Faulkner [p.92] →

'Phantom Rose' wallpaper, 1958
Audrey Levy [p.28] →

## Lighting

In the early years of the scheme, award-winning light fittings tended to be traditional pendants for domestic use. The emphasis was on quality of materials and detailing, as in the brass fittings of the 'Satina' pendant by Nigel Chapman, and the unusual coloured glass shades of the 'Chelsea' pendant by Richard Stevens and Peter Rodd. From the mid-1960s on, however, spotlights, display fittings and lighting tracks were frequent winners, reflecting the general shift in the awards' focus away from the purely domestic sphere towards public spaces and engineering solutions.

Throughout the period covered by the awards scheme, awards for lighting were dominated by the large firms of Rotaflex and Concord (which eventually merged), and Atlas Lighting. The most prominent designers of light fittings were the husband-and-wife team John and Sylvia Reid, and product and furniture designer Robert Heritage, all honoured with awards for their lighting as well as in other fields of design.

*'Satina' pendant light fitting, 1958*
Nigel Chapman [p.29] →

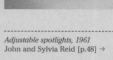

*Adjustable spotlights, 1961*
John and Sylvia Reid [p.48] →

# *1959* Planit

*'Planit' wall tiles*
Designed by Derek Hodgkinson
for H. & R. Johnson Ltd, 1958

# *1959* Malindi

*'Malindi' furnishing fabric*
Designed by Gwenfred Jarvis
for Liberty & Co., 1957

# *1959* Flamingo

*'Flamingo' easy chair*
Designed by Ernest Race for
Race Furniture Ltd, 1959

Award-Winning British Design

1957 — 1988

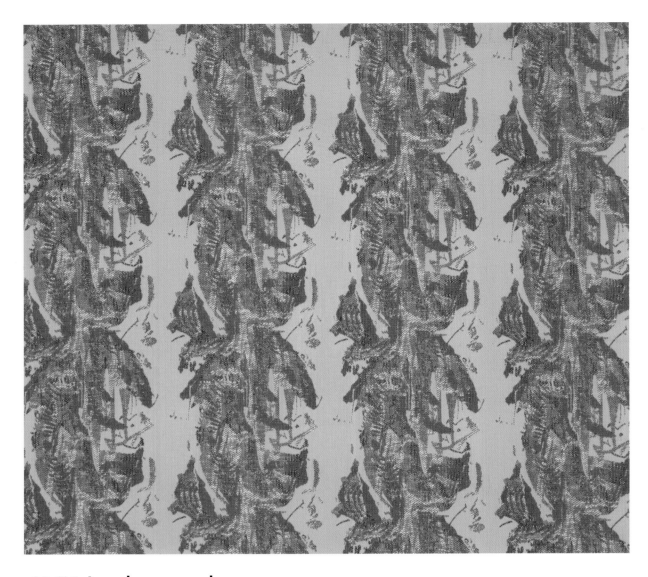

## *1959* Inglewood

*'Inglewood' furnishing fabric*
Designed by Humphrey Spender
for Edinburgh Weavers, 1958

# *1959* Ellipse

*'Ellipse' pendant light fitting*
Designed by Paul Boissevain
for Merchant Adventurers
Ltd, 1959

# *1959* Mandala

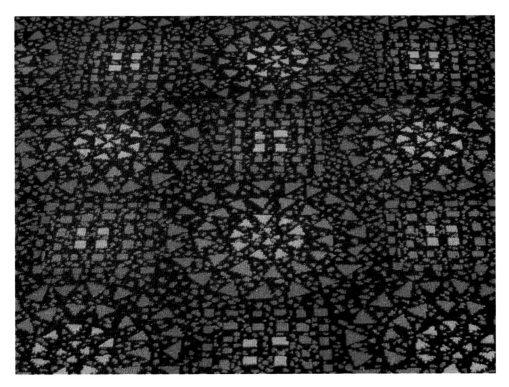

*'Mandala' Wilton carpet*
Designed by Audrey Tanner
for Carpet Manufacturing Co.
Ltd, 1958

# *1960* Bouquet Garni

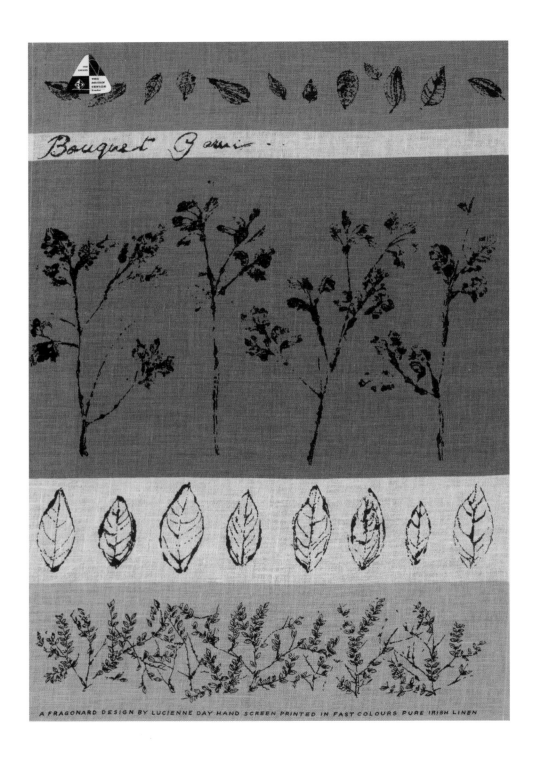

A FRAGONARD DESIGN BY LUCIENNE DAY HAND SCREEN PRINTED IN FAST COLOURS PURE IRISH LINEN

*'Bouquet Garni' glass towel*
One of three designs by Lucienne Day
for Thomas Somerset & Co. Ltd, 1959

*'Chelsea' pendant light fittings*
Designed by Richard Stevens and
Peter Rodd for Atlas Lighting Ltd,
with shades made by James Powell
& Son (Whitefriars) Ltd, 1959

*1960* Chelsea

# *1960* Street lighting

Street lighting
The CoID exhibition of street furniture at the
Southbank, London, 1960–61, included street lighting
columns and lanterns designed by Richard Stevens,
manufactured by Abacus Engineering Ltd for Atlas
Lighting Ltd

## *1960* Anniversary Ware

---

*Casserole dish*
From the 'Anniversary Ware' range of tableware
designed by John and Sylvia Reid for Izons & Co.
Ltd, 1960

# *1960* Queensberry Ware

*Plate*
From the 'Queensberry Ware' range of nursery
tableware, shape designed by David Queensberry,
pattern designed by Bernard Blatch for Crown
Staffordshire China Co. Ltd, 1960

# *1961* Cormorant

*'Cormorant' folding outdoor chair*
Designed by Ernest Race for Race
Furniture Ltd, 1961

# *1961* Spotlights

*Adjustable spotlights*
Designed by John and Sylvia Reid
for Rotaflex (Great Britain) Ltd, 1961

# *1961* Rio TR70

---
*'Rio TR70' transistor radio*
Designed by Eric Marshall for Ultra Radio
& Television Ltd, 1961

# *1962* Sunflower

*'Sunflower' furnishing fabric*
Designed by Howard Carter for Heal Fabrics
Ltd, 1962

# *1962* Trifoliate

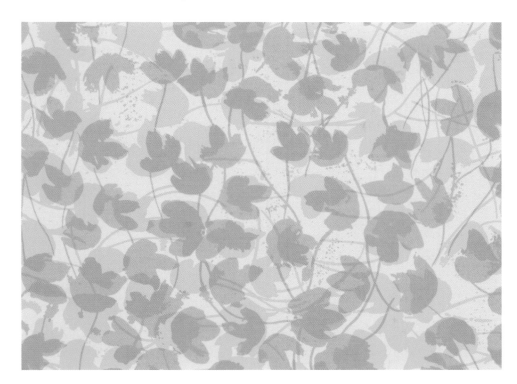

*'Trifoliate' wallpaper*
From the 'Palladio 5' range
of wallpapers, designed by
Cliff Holden for The Wall
Paper Manufacturers Ltd, 1962

# *1962* Tiles

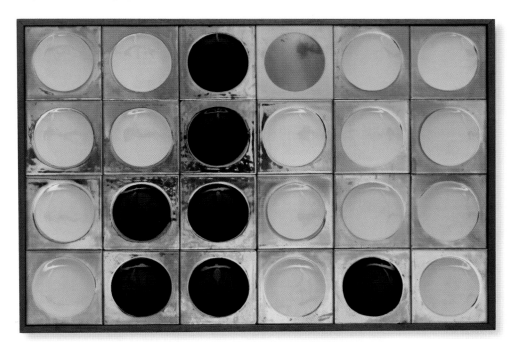

*Dimpled wall tiles*
Designed by Michael Caddy
for Wade Architectural
Ceramics, 1962

# *1963* Cruachan

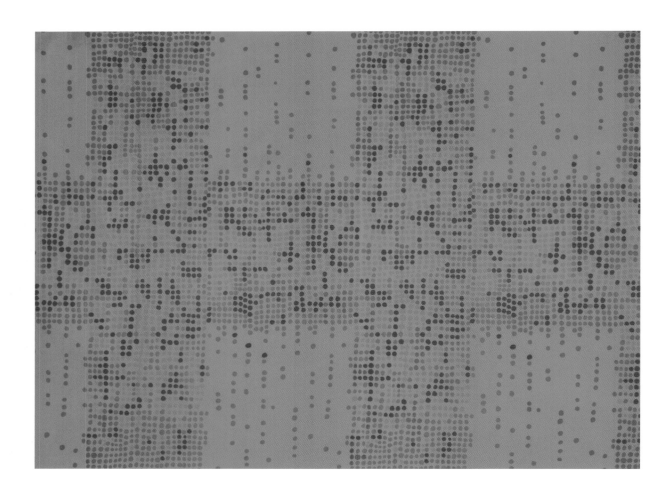

----------------------------------

*'Cruachan' furnishing fabric*
Designed by Peter McCulloch
for Hull Traders Ltd, 1963

# *1963* Courier

-----------------------------------
*'Courier' cordless electric shaver*
Designed by Kenneth Grange
for Henry Milward & Sons, 1963

# *1964* Division

'Division' furnishing fabric
Designed by Shirley Craven
for Hull Traders Ltd, 1964

# *1964* Brownie Vecta

*'Brownie Vecta' camera*
Designed by Kenneth Grange
with company design staff at
Kodak Ltd, 1964

# *1964* Doorbell kit

*Electric doorbell kit*
From a range of electric
doorbells and fittings, designed
by Norman Stevenson with
company design staff at
V. & E. Friedland Ltd, 1964

# *1964* Mitre and Harlequin

*'Mitre' vase with 'Harlequin'
bowl and centrepiece*
From a range of tableware
designed by David
Queensberry for Webb
Corbett Ltd, 1963

# *1964* Insulated tumblers

*Insulated tumblers*
Designed by H.D.F. Creighton
for Insulex Ltd, 1962

# *1965* Mark II

# *1965* Legend

*'Legend' furnishing fabric*
Designed by Alan Reynolds
for Edinburgh Weavers, 1962

# *1965* Polyanna

*'Polyanna' rag doll*
From a range of rag dolls
designed by Joy and Malcolm
Wilcox for Sari Fabrics Ltd, 1965

# *1965* Alveston

------------------------------

*Fork and spoon*
From the 'Alveston' range of
cutlery designed by Robert
Welch for Old Hall Tableware
Ltd, 1961

# *1965* Embassy

------------------------------

*Teapot and jug*
From the 'Embassy' range
of silverware designed and
manufactured by David Mellor
for British embassies, 1960

# *1966* Brooch

*Brooch*
From a range of jewellery
designed and made
by Andrew Grima for
H.J. Company Ltd, 1966

# *1966* Barbican

*'Barbican' hand basin*
Designed by Chamberlin,
Powell & Bon with company
design staff under Munroe
Blair at Twyfords, 1966

# *1966* Hamilton

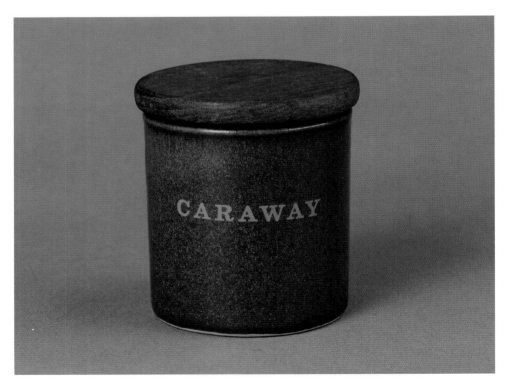

*Spice jar*
From the 'Hamilton' range
designed by D. Tarquin Cole
and John Minshaw for
Govancroft Potteries Ltd, 1966

# *1966* Model 1108

*'Model 1108' mono
radio receiver*
Designed by Robin Day
and Douglas Jones for
Pye of Cambridge Ltd, 1966

# *1966* STC Deltaphone

*'STC Deltaphone' telephone*
Designed by Martyn Rowlands
with STC engineers at Standard
Telephones and Cables Ltd, 1966

*1967* Road signs

----------------------------------------
*Road signs*
Graphic system designed by Margaret Calvert and
Jock Kinneir for the Ministry of Transport, 1967

# *1967* Tempest

--------------------------------------------------

*'Tempest' racing yacht*
Designed by Ian Proctor for Richardson
Boats & Plastics Ltd, 1967

*1968* Nova

*Jugs*
From the 'Nova' range of tableware designed by
David Harman Powell for Ekco Plastics Ltd, 1967

# *1968* Kompas 1

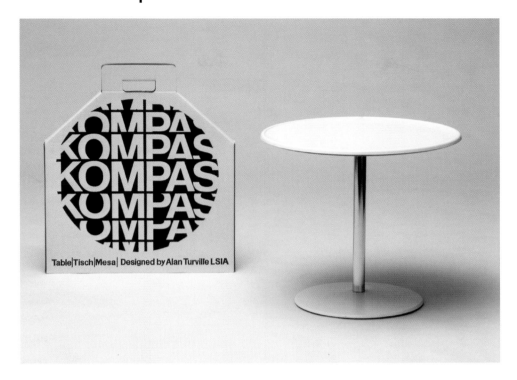

'Kompas 1' self-assembly
occasional table
Designed by Alan Turville
for S. Hille & Co. Ltd, 1967

# *1968* Trilateral

'Trilateral' poster display unit
Designed by Ronald Denton for
London and Provincial Poster
Group Ltd, 1967

# *1968* Chair Thing

*'Chair Thing'*
From the 'Those Things' range of self-assembly
children's furniture, designed by Peter Murdoch
for Perspective Designs Ltd, 1968

## Tableware

From the 1950s to the 1980s consumers' changing approaches to dining were reflected in tableware design, and resulted in increasingly informal styles, modern materials and oven-to-table cookware. David Mellor and Robert Welch both trained as silversmiths but were instrumental in establishing the popularity of stainless steel tableware in Britain. Mellor was appointed as design consultant at Walker & Hall in 1954, and was central to its move from silver into stainless steel. He later became the first cutlery designer to combine stainless steel with acetal resin handles. Welch was inspired by Scandinavian design during visits to the region as a student, and in 1955 he became consultant to Old Hall, then Britain's only producer of stainless steel tableware.

One of the most important ceramic designers of the post-war period was David Queensberry, who began a long-standing design partnership with Martin Hunt in 1966. Their award-winning works reflect the widespread shift away from bone china towards more robust stoneware during the 1960s and '70s. Another important change in the use of materials was the growth in plastic tableware. Midwinter Pottery extended their business into this new area by collaborating with the firm British Industrial Plastics. Another innovator in the field was Ekco Plastics, where David Harman Powell became chief designer in 1960. The success of Harman Powell's 'Nova' range led to his appointment as the first ICI Tutor in Plastics at the Royal College of Art.

'Queensberry Ware' plate, 1960
Bernard Blatch and David Queensberry
[p.46] →

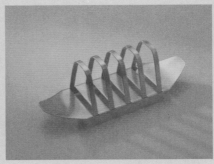

'Old Hall' toast rack, 1956
Robert Welch [p.30] →

## Product Design

Product design can encompass a wide range of objects, from household appliances and garden tools to office equipment. Probably the best-known post-war British product designer is Kenneth Grange, a founding partner of the Pentagram design consultancy. Grange began his career as a drafting assistant in an architecture practice, exemplifying how product and industrial designers often entered the field from other backgrounds. He went on to design everything from the 'Kenwood Chef' food processor to the 'InterCity 125' train, and won awards for a wide variety of everyday objects and appliances.

Specialist training in product design was introduced in Britain in the mid-twentieth century. Martyn Rowlands specialized in plastics on the first three-year industrial design course at the Central School of Arts and Crafts. He worked for Bakelite and then set up the design department at Ekco Plastics, before going freelance in 1959. The lightweight, wall-mountable 'Deltaphone' and 'Deltaline' telephones of 1966 are among his most iconic designs.

Many of the award-winning products in this category were innovations by small specialist companies or independent inventors. For example, Ron Hickman, a car designer with a day job at Lotus, developed the immensely successful 'Workmate' workbench at home following a DIY accident. He spent several years trying to persuade manufacturers to produce it before Black & Decker eventually took it up with great success.

*'Courier' cordless electric shaver, 1963*
Kenneth Grange [p.53] →

*'STC Deltaphone' telephone, 1966*
Martyn Rowlands [p.63] →

## Toys

The whimsical aspects of British design culture are perhaps most evident in the award-winning toys. Many winners, including Joy and Malcolm Wilcox's rag dolls and Edward Harvey's 'Polydron', began as kitchen-table enterprises before going into large-scale commercial production. In his range of toys for Trendon, Patrick Rylands was able to indulge in almost pure design, without regard for function. At 27, the youngest ever winner of the Duke of Edinburgh's Prize for Elegant Design, Rylands created the 'Gyrosphere' and the 'Bird' and 'Fish' bath toys, a series of captivating objects with no other purpose than to inspire children's imaginations.

The increasing provision of public play areas in the post-war decades brought about a variety of imaginative designs for playground equipment. In 1972 the Design Council began to compile an index of well-designed playground equipment for local authorities, and its award to SMP (Landscapes) Ltd that year reflected its official interest in this field. SMP were particularly commended for their attention to safety features, including swing seats made from rubber tyres rather than unforgiving plastic or wood.

'Polyanna' rag doll, 1965
Joy and Malcolm Wilcox [p.59] →

'Fish' and 'Bird' bath toys, 1969
Patrick Rylands [p.77] →

## Jewellery

In 1966 the Duke of Edinburgh's Prize for Elegant Design was awarded for the first time to a collection of one-off handmade objects, rather than an industrial product. The winner was jeweller Andrew Grima, a favourite of the royal family, and Prince Philip purchased a brooch from the winning collection as a gift for the Queen. The award recognized the renaissance in British jewellery design that had taken place since 1960, following the reduction of the high purchase tax imposed on jewellery after the war.

Wendy Ramshaw was the second jeweller to win an award, for a collection of pieces that included sets of stacking rings displayed on elegant cylindrical acrylic mounts. Ramshaw first designed these mounts for the award winners' exhibition at the Design Centre in 1972, and they went on to become an iconic part of her design practice, taking on increasingly complex geometric forms.

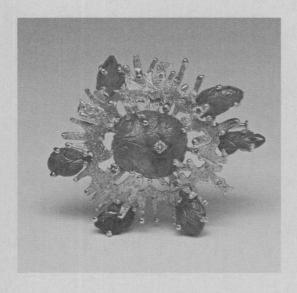

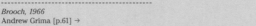

*Brooch, 1966*
Andrew Grima [p.61] →

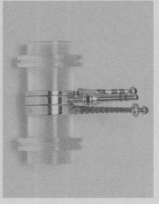

*Rings, 1971*
Wendy Ramshaw [p.81] →

# *1968* Complex

'*Complex' furnishing fabric*
Designed by Barbara Brown
for Heal Fabrics Ltd, 1967

# *1969* Bollard light

*Bollard light*
Designed by P.E. Pizzey and
H.G. Davies for Frederick
Thomas & Co., 1968

# *1969* QE2 chairs

*Restaurant chairs for the QE2*
Designed by Robert Heritage
for Race Furniture Ltd, 1968

# *1970* Spiral

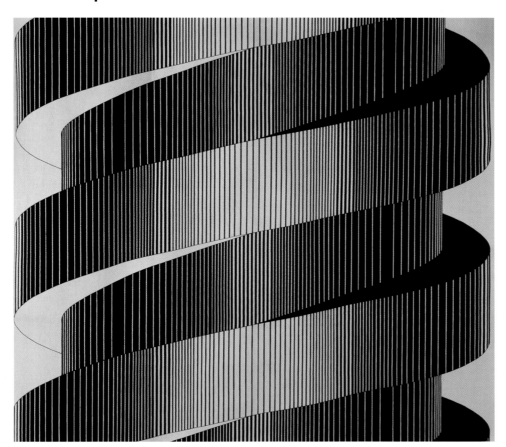

*'Spiral' furnishing fabric*
Designed by Barbara Brown
for Heal Fabrics Ltd, 1969

# *1970* Neptune

*'Neptune' lamp*
From a range of lamps
designed by Martin Hunt
and James Kirkwood for
JRM Design Sales Ltd, 1970

# *1970* Wentworth

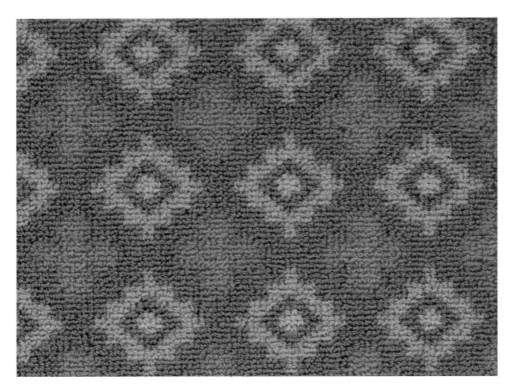

*'Wentworth' Brussels carpet*
From the 'Kensington' range
of carpets designed by David
Hicks with company designers
Colin Royle and John Palmer
for John Crossley & Sons
Ltd, 1969

# *1970* Fish and Bird

*'Fish' and 'Bird' bath toys*
From a range of toys designed by
Patrick Rylands for Trendon Ltd, 1969

# *1971* Globoot

*'Globoot' children's waterproof boots*
Designed by Globoot Footwear
for Plastic Coatings Ltd, 1971

# *1971* Teltron

-------------------------------------------------
*'Teltron' atomic physics teaching aids*
Designed by Derek Power and Dennis Beard
with Noel Haring Associates for Teltron Ltd, 1970

# *1972* Variset

Hat, coat and umbrella stand
From the 'Variset' range of hat
and coat hooks, designed by
Kenneth Grange for A.J. Binns
Ltd, 1971

# *1972* Playground equipment

*Children's playground equipment*
Designed and manufactured by
SMP (Landscapes) Ltd, 1972

# *1972* Interchangeable

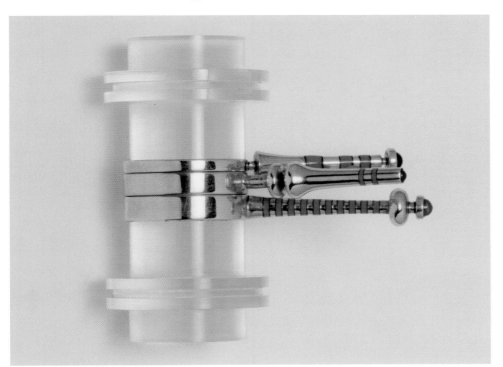

*Rings*
From the 'Interchangeable'
range of jewellery designed
and made by Wendy Ramshaw,
1971

# *1972* Jars

*Storage jars*
From a range of kitchen and
table glassware designed by
Frank Thrower for Dartington
Glass Ltd, 1972

# *1972* Tiles

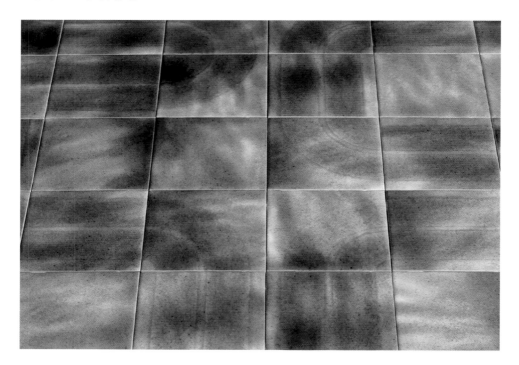

*Wall and floor tiles*
From a range of tiles designed
by Sally Anderson for Sally
Anderson (Ceramics) Ltd, 1972

# *1973* Garden netting

*Garden netting*
Designed by Brian Mercer for
Netlon Ltd, 1972

# *1973* Bida

*'Bida' upholstery fabric*
From a range of fabrics
designed and manufactured by
Sekers Fabrics Ltd, 1973

# *1973* Wharfedale Isodynamic

-------------------------------------------
*'Wharfedale Isodynamic' headphones*
Designed by Oliver Hill with the Rank
Radio Industrial Design Unit for
Rank Radio International Ltd, 1972

# *1973* Workmate Mark 2

*'Workmate Mark 2' workbench*
Designed by Ron Hickman for
Black & Decker Ltd, 1972

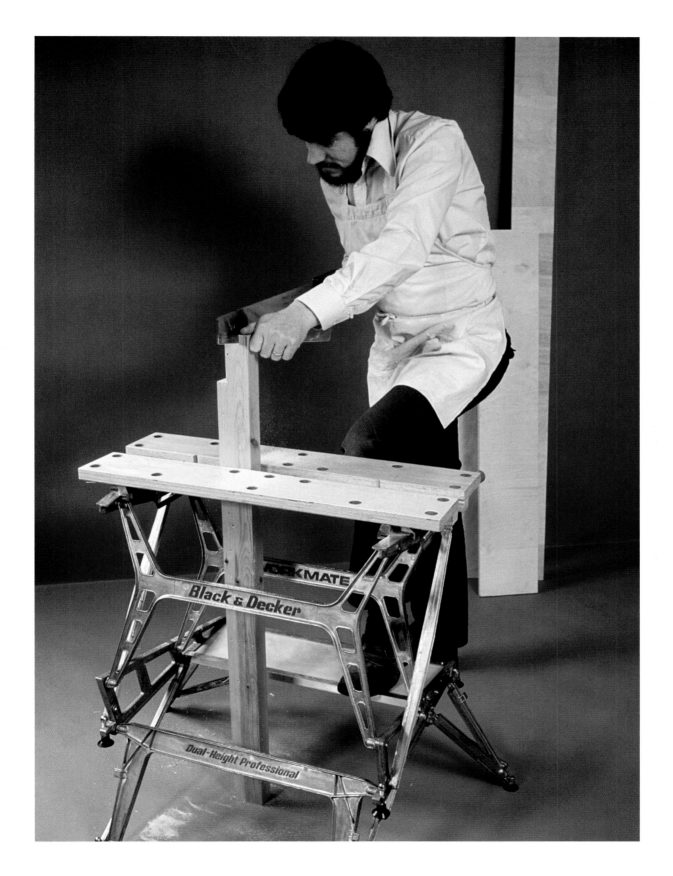

# *1974* Sorbo-Ski

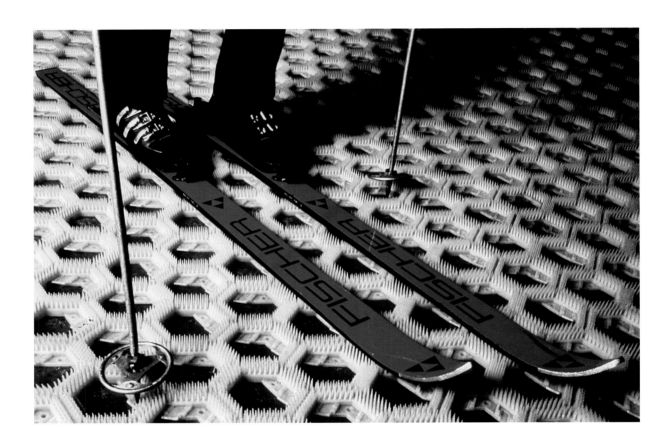

-------------------------------------------------
*'Sorbo-Ski' artificial ski slope*
Designed by John Blandford Jupe and
Roy L. Manns for Summer Ski Ltd, 1973

# *1974* **700** range

------------------------------------------------

*'700 range' chairs and tables*
Designed by David Mellor for Abacus
Municipal Ltd, 1973

# *1974* AC1 and AP1

*'AC1' and 'AP1' pre-amplifier
and power amplifier*
Designed by Robert Stuart
and Allen Boothroyd for
Lecson Audio Ltd, 1973

# *1974* Super-Jet

*'4834 Super-Jet 12' dishwasher*
Designed by Paul Moss and
Cedric Mastin for Hoover
Ltd, 1974

# *1975* Display rack

*Periodical display rack*
Designed by John Marshall
for Marico Furniture Ltd, 1974

# *1975* Brix

'Brix' curtain fabric
Designed by Anna Caldwell for Margo
International Fabrics Ltd, 1975

# *1975* Contrast

*Coffee pot*
From the 'Contrast' range of tableware, designed
by Martin Hunt for Hornsea Pottery Co. Ltd, 1975

# *1976* Kelpie

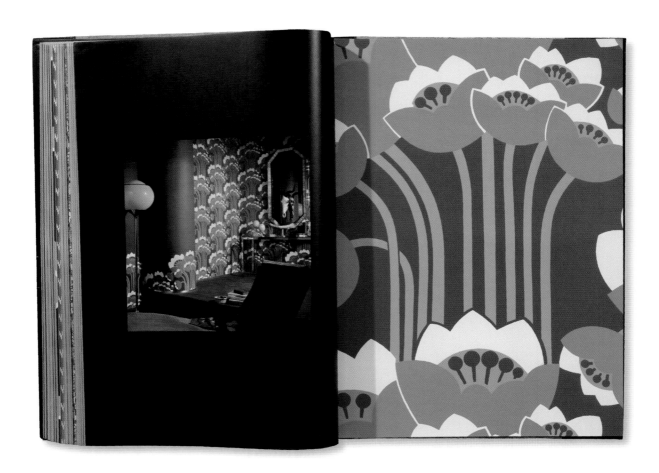

*'Kelpie' wallpaper*
From the 'Studio One' Vymura range of
wallpapers, designed by Sue Faulkner
for ICI Ltd (Paints Division), 1976

# *1976* Euclid

*'Euclid' carpet*
From the 'Good Companions' range of Axminster carpets and rugs, designed and manufactured by David Bartle for Broadloom Carpets Ltd, 1976

# *1976* Waltham

*'Waltham' kitchen*
A stand in the Design Centre featuring the 'Waltham' range of kitchen units, designed by Nigel V. Walters for Wrighton International Furniture, 1976

# *1977* Topper

*'Topper' sailing dinghy*
Designed by Ian Proctor for
J.V. Dunhill Boats Ltd, 1976

# *1977* Concept

*Teapot, milk jug and cup*
From the 'Concept' range
of tableware designed by
Martin Hunt and Colin Bentley
Rawson for Hornsea Pottery
Co. Ltd, 1977

# *1977* Chinese Ivory

*Spoon, fork and table knife*
From the 'Chinese Ivory'
range of cutlery designed
and manufactured by
David Mellor, 1975

## *1977* Sovereign

*'Sovereign' calculator*
Designed by John Pemberton, John Holland and
Victor Thomas for Sinclair Radionics Ltd, 1976

# *1978* Microvision

--------------------------------------------------
*'Microvision' pocket television*
Designed by John Pemberton and company
designers at Sinclair Radionics Ltd, 1978

# *1978* Micro

*'Micro' folding bicycle*
Designed by Peter Radnall
for Micro Cycles Ltd, 1978

# *1979* Tinker Tramp

'Tinker Tramp' inflatable dinghy
Designed by Fred Benyon-
Tinker for J.M. Henshaw
(Marine) Ltd, 1979

# *1980* Amstad

*'Amstad' perch seating*
Designed by David Goodwin,
Peter Wheeler and Andrew
Smyth for Amstad Systems
Ltd, 1980

# *1982* Supporto

*'Supporto' office chair*
Designed by Fred Scott for
Hille International Ltd, 1979

# *1982* Mark IV

*'Mark IV' racing scull*
Designed by G.A.S. Locke and
S.J. Adcock for Glyn Locke
(Racing Shells) Ltd, 1982

*'ZX81' personal computer*
Designed by Rick Dickinson, manufactured by
Timex Corporation for Sinclair Research Ltd, 1981

# *1984* Côte d'Azur

*'Côte d'Azur' furnishing fabric*
From the 'Six Views' range of
fabrics designed by Susan
Collier and Sarah Campbell
for Collier Campbell Ltd, 1983

# *1984* Tran-Sit

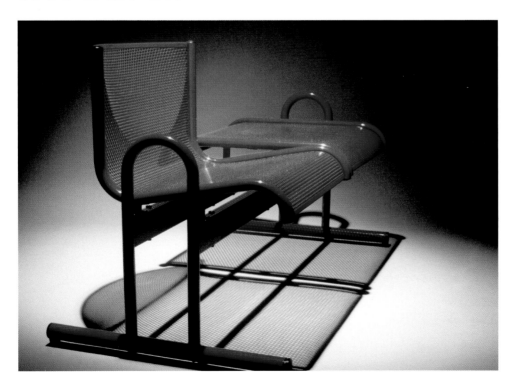

*'Tran-Sit' public seating*
Designed by Rodney Kinsman
and Peter Glynn Smith for
OMK Design Ltd, 1984

# *1985* Polydron 3D

'Polydron 3D' geometric toy
Designed by Edward and Ronan Harvey
for Polydron Ltd, 1984

## Audiovisual and Electronic Equipment

In its early years, the CoID tended to focus on the styling of audiovisual equipment and recognized such products as Eric Marshall's minimalist 'TR70' transistor radio with awards. Later technical developments came to play a stronger role, showcasing the strength of British hi-fi design and manufacturing. The Yorkshire company Wharfedale, a leading innovator in loudspeaker technology since the early 1930s, won an award in 1973 for its 'Isodynamic' headphones. They were the first commercially available orthodynamic headphones and offered high-quality sound reproduction at a much lower price than had previously been possible.

The inventor Clive Sinclair was behind a number of award-winning electronic products. His 'Microvision' black-and-white portable television used a revolutionary two-inch cathode-ray tube, developed exclusively for Sinclair Radionics by Telefunken. However, the television's innovative features outstripped its consumer appeal, and it made a loss, leading to the collapse of Sinclair Radionics. Sinclair went on to establish a new company, Science of Cambridge, which would develop highly influential early home computers. His 'ZX81' computer, which won an award in 1982, was an updated version of the 'ZX80', the first home computer available in the UK for under £100. The accessibility of Sinclair machines was a significant factor in the rapid growth of the home computer market — the UK led the world in home computer ownership throughout the 1980s.

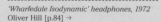

*'Wharfedale Isodynamic' headphones, 1972*
Oliver Hill [p.84] →

*'ZX81' personal computer, 1981*
Rick Dickinson [p.102] →

## Transport

The consumer goods category of the awards scheme included forms of transport associated with leisure activities, including sailing, rowing and cycling. Motor vehicles were placed in a separate category. Marine engineering is a traditional British design strength, and boats were well represented among the award winners. The leading designer in the field was Ian Proctor, whose award-winning designs include his innovative 'Topper' sailing dinghy. The plastic hull of the 'Topper' is moulded in just two sections, making it affordable, strong and light. It remains extremely popular today.

The 'Moulton' bicycle was the first to pair small wheels with a full-size frame. Engineer Alex Moulton had a background in automotive and aeronautical design, and had previously worked on the innovative rubber suspension system of the Mini. The Moulton's combination of high-pressure tyres and small wheels minimizes rolling resistance and drag, thereby allowing the cyclist to go faster with less effort.

'Topper' sailing dinghy, 1976
Ian Proctor [p.94] →

'Moulton Stowaway' bicycle, 1964
Alex Moulton [p.16] →

## Public Spaces

The CoID attempted to improve the appearance of Britain's public spaces by publishing a biennial catalogue of street furniture, distributed for free to every local authority in the country. One of the most important designers in this field was David Mellor, who moved beyond his initial training as a silversmith to produce such iconic designs as the British traffic-light system. Another influential figure was Rodney Kinsman, the founder of OMK Design, which specialized in contract furniture. The British Airports Authority commissioned his 'Tran-Sit' seating system for Gatwick Airport in 1984, and it was subsequently purchased by a wide range of clients, from the Metropolitan Police to hospitals around the country.

Between 1957 and 1967, Jock Kinneir and Margaret Calvert redesigned all of Britain's road signs, starting with the new motorways. Their aim was to create signs that were easy to read and understand while driving at speed. This hugely ambitious project meant that, for the first time, the lettering, colours, shapes and symbols on all signs were coordinated. Kinneir and Calvert's designs became models for countries all over the world.

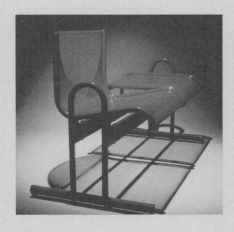

'Tran-Sit' public seating, 1984
Rodney Kinsman [p.103] →

Road signs, 1967
Margaret Calvert and Jock Kinneir [p.64] →

## Further Reading

Full descriptions of winning products were published each year in *Design*, the magazine of the Design Council. *Design* has been digitized for the period 1965—74 and is freely available online through the Visual Arts Data Service (VADS), at www.vads.ac.uk.

The Design Council Archive is housed in the Design Archives at the University of Brighton. It includes extensive records of the awards scheme, as well as all other aspects of the Council's work. Photographs from the Design Council Archive are also accessible online through VADS.

The Design Council Slide Collection is held by Manchester Metropolitan University; the majority of the collection has been digitized and is also available through VADS. It includes images of almost all of the award-winning designs.

The V&A Archive includes information on the acquisition of the award-winning objects, as well as correspondence between the CoID and the V&A, and other records relating to the Circulation Department.

## Acknowledgements

The author would like to thank the following people for their assistance and support: Lesley Whitworth and Catherine Moriarty of the Design Council Archive at the University of Brighton; Nigel Campbell, Head of Communications at the Design Council; Trevor Grubb, former Head of Exhibitions at the Design Centre; Jennifer Opie, formerly of the V&A's Circulation Department; John Davis, Visual Resources Curator at Manchester Metropolitan University and custodian of the Design Council Slide Collection; the book's designers, Lee Davies and Paul Reardon of Peter & Paul; Laura Potter and Clare Davis of V&A Publishing; Ghislaine Wood and Christopher Breward, curators of the exhibition *British Design 1948—2012: Innovation in the Modern Age*; Pauline Goodlad of the V&A's Documentation and Collections Management Services department; and project interns Kathryn Braganza, Hannah Gregory, Katy Houston, Harriet Louth and Gabriel Williams, who gave their time to assist with research and cataloguing.